TRANSACTIONS

of the

American Philosophical Society

Held at Philadelphia for Promoting Useful Knowledge

VOLUME 83, Part 6

From Defense to Resistance: Justification of Violence during the French Wars of Religion

Kathleen A. Parrow

Department of History and
Social Science
Black Hills State University

AMERICAN PHILOSOPHICAL SOCIETY

Independence Square Philadelphia

Library of Congress Catalog
Card Number 93–72130
International Standard Book Number 0-87169-836-6
US ISSN 0065-9746

CONTENTS

ACKNOWLEDGMENTS

This monograph originated a few years ago as a Ph.D. dissertation at the University of Rochester and has undergone numerous metamorphoses since its completion in that form in 1985. Although the central thesis has remained essentially unchanged over the years, the supporting material, both primary and secondary, has been expanded even as the length has been shortened (a trick I am unable to understand and probably unable to repeat) and the legal arguments have been greatly clarified as a result. I could not have done this alone.

My interest in legal history dates back to my choice of a Masters thesis topic at the University of Wisconsin-Milwaukee, where James Brundage and Roland Stromberg provided direction for my work on the legal humanist Etienne Pasquier, and my friend and fellow graduate student Elizabeth Makowski shared with me her enthusiasm for scholarship in general and canon law in particular. Early inspiration for the immediate topic at hand emerged from graduate seminars in the History Department at the University of Rochester, which also provided some of the funding for work on the original dissertation. The constructive criticism and inspiration provided there by Donald Kelley and Richard Kaeuper were useful then and continue to be so, even on those occasions when I ignore their suggestions. My friends and colleagues, especially those where I have taught, also deserve my thanks for their fresh insights and support of my research which in many cases is far outside their own. My special thanks go to Sarah Hanley, who has given so much of her time to so many of us, and to the readers and editorial staff at the American Philosophical Society, whose suggestions have greatly improved an earlier draft of this manuscript.

Parts of this work have appeared as an article "Neither Treason nor Heresy: Use of Defense Arguments to Avoid Forfeiture during the French Wars of Religion," in the Winter 1991 issue of *The Sixteenth Century Journal* and as papers presented at the Missouri Valley History Conference (Omaha 1989) and the Sixteenth Century Studies Conference (Philadelphia 1991). Additional thanks go to the Faculty Research Committee at Black Hills State University, which provided the funding which allowed me to spend the summer of 1992 in Iowa City revising this manuscript. As important as the intellectual and financial support, and perhaps more so, has been the help furnished to me by librarians and interlibrary loan offices as I have moved around the country: the University of Rochester, Appalachian State University (Boone, North Carolina), the University of Iowa, and at Black Hills State University (Spearfish, South Dakota). Their help in obtaining sources has been invaluable and I could not have completed this project without them.

I dedicate this volume to the memory of my fellow Rochester graduates Bernard McLane, Sheila Kamerick, and John D'Amico, respected friends and scholars who have left us much too soon.

Iowa City
July 1993

* * * *

AUTHOR'S NOTE

Spelling, accents, capitalization, and punctuation of pamphlet titles follow the copy and edition used as closely as possible. Since more than one edition of many of these pamphlets exists, reference numbers are included to *French Political Pamphlets 1547–1648: A Catalog of Major Collections in American Libraries*, edited by Robert O. Lindsay and John Neu.

Inconsistent spelling is a common characteristic of sixteenth-century works. These variations are retained throughout, but in the bibliography they are ignored for purposes of alphabetization. For example, "Edit" and "Edict" are treated as the same word and pamphlets beginning with those words are alphabetized as though they were spelled the same.

INTRODUCTION

The right to defend oneself and one's property developed in part from the ancient Roman and medieval legal concept allowing the use of violence to repel violence. This justification of defensive violence for the individual later formed the basis for the early modern political concept of using violence to resist tyranny. This latter development was complex and was based in large part on the legal arguments of French politico-legal writers during the sixteenth-century Wars of Religion. One of the aspects of works written on this topic which has been largely ignored by modern writers is the emphasis on law. Sixteenth-century authors supported a wide variety of responses (ranging from passive tolerance of oppression to tyrannicide and warfare) with carefully supported legal justifications drawn from actual law or from a historical myth of the past that claimed to have a legal basis in the popular mind. Such ideas as popular sovereignty and royal election, as well as just war, developed from Roman law in the Middle Ages and became increasingly familiar as a basis for resistance theory in the sixteenth century.

Resistance theory has been discussed often in terms of public law and political thought, and the just war arguments of the medieval churchmen and of later Catholic and Protestant writers have been used frequently as background to twentieth-century just war arguments. The general milieu of social violence, especially from the Middle Ages to the mid-seventeenth century, has also been discussed by numerous authors. Following is a brief, though by no means comprehensive, survey of some of those works most relevant to this essay. It will become obvious to the reader that what they generally lack is the understanding of the legal basis, distinct from the political, religious, or social basis, which was an essential element in the justification developed in resistance theories.

Political Theory

The trend in historical scholarship for a number of years has been away from studies devoted to political thought, but older

1

studies in this area, including works by John W. Allen, Vittorio
de Caprariis, William F. Church, Pierre Mesnard, and Georges
Weill are still useful.[1] Even though some parts of these works
have become outdated or superseded by new research, they remain excellent discussions of constitutional theory and practice,
but they are almost purely political in orientation. As political
theory, their authors' interests in law remained focused on public, constitutional law. They ignored the importance of other legal
elements, such as private and canon (church) law, in the development and application of political theories, even when they acknowledged that practicing jurists made important contributions
to the development of those theories.

John W. Allen's *A History of Political Thought in the Sixteenth Century*, although written in the 1920s, is still a comprehensive work
which surveys the political importance of Lutheran and Calvinist
thought in England, France, and Italy. Allen perceived a psycho-
logical change in Europe which preceded the more formal political change; the reformation resulted in the triumph of secular
authority over the church in their centuries-old struggle. He felt
that the traditional independence of the provincial and municipal
authorities, combined with the lawlessness and ambition of the
nobles, became allied with Protestantism. This alliance posed a
threat to the centralizing efforts of the monarchies and ultimately
resulted in civil wars. The opposing forces first countered monarchical claims with constitutional claims of their own, then
with claims of popular sovereignty, and finally with claims of a
right to rebel.[2]

The three stages in the development of sixteenth-century Protestant political thought which Allen outlined are still useful: the
general acceptance of a religious doctrine of non-resistance to
constitutional authority; the appearance of the Genevan political
ideal; and the justification of armed resistance, which he dates as
beginning between 1550 and 1560. This latter stage depended entirely on the local circumstances. In areas where the sovereign
supported the Calvinists, they continued to preach non-
resistance. This is born out in the case of France, where non-

---

[1]John William Allen, *A History of Political Thought in the Sixteenth Century* (New York:
Dial Press, Inc., 1928); Vittorio de Caprariis, *Propaganda e pensiero politico in Francia durante
le guerre di religione*, v. 1, *1559–1572* (Naples: Edizioni scientifiche italiane, 1959); William
Farr Church, *Constitutional Thought in Sixteenth-Century France: A Study in the Evolution of
Ideas* (Cambridge: Harvard University Press, 1941); Pierre Mesnard, *L'essor de la philosophie
politique au XVIe siècle*, 3rd ed. (Paris: J. Vrin, 1969); and Georges Weill, *Les théories sur le
pouvoir royal en France pendant les guerres de religion* (Paris: 1891; Rp. Geneva: Slatkine Reprints, 1971).
[2]Allen, xiii-xv.

resistance was preached until the Huguenots felt the need and the strength to resist effectively. At that point, new theories were applied, even though they ran counter to Calvin's teachings.[3]

Allen's discussion of the Catholic League writers and pamphleteers remains generally solid, but understandably shows its age in light of several decades of new research and methodologies. This is also obvious in his presentation of the Huguenot writers. He gave a thorough explication of their major works in the development towards resistance theory, including the *Francogallia*, the *Reveille-Matin*, the *Vindiciae contre tyrannos*, the collection of Huguenot writings in the *Mémoires de l'Estat de France sous Charles IX*, and the works of Jean Bodin, but he emphasized that the theory of the *Vindiciae* was medieval rather than Protestant and he considered Hotman's *Francogallia* greatly overrated, on the grounds that its placement of ultimate sovereignty in the community as a whole was not a new idea.[4] That the arguments in these two important works were not new may well be one of their most important elements, as more recent scholarship and new critical editions of important works continue to demonstrate. Many of the increasingly radical ideas presented to justify violent resistance and rebellion in the sixteenth-century were familiar ones to contemporaries. They were often presented in new ways, with new implications, but the underpinnings were recognizable, very often based on legal theory and practice as much as on political theory, and for that very reason they were more readily acceptable to their audiences.

In his 1935 work *L'essor de la philosophie politique au XVIe siècle*, Pierre Mesnard emphasized the effect of the social group and social milieu on political thinkers and the uncertainty of establishing universal ideas independent of their experiences. This represents the dilemma between empiricism and speculation, observation and theory. Philosophers, he said, try to conceptualize one global, indivisible society, but society is more complex.[5] To him the most serious political problem of the time seemed to be the coordination of the social groups among themselves and the exact understanding of their relationship to the state. He saw society not as external to its members, but as alive in their cooperation, and underneath there was a real unity, despite the different surface patterns.[6]

---

[3] Ibid., 52–60 for Calvin's teachings on non-resistance.
[4] Ibid., 303–310.
[5] Mesnard, 1–2.
[6] Ibid., 3.

After discussing the earlier religious movements, Mesnard considered the political aspects of Calvinism and the works of Théodore de Bèze and François Hotman, and the *Vindiciae* and its emphasis on popular sovereignty and the magistrates as the proper persons to exercise this sovereignty when necessary.[7] Mesnard also considered other standard works, such as the *Reveille-Matin* and the *De Jure Regni apud Scotos;* the theories of universal religion, universal law, and universal monarchy; and eventually Jean Bodin's *La République.* In the latter work he singled out for attention Bodin's distinction between law and contract: law is a unilateral act manifesting authority and contract is an agreement between two parties.[8] Mesnard concluded that the group whose profession operated at the median between theory and observation (or philosophy and science) was the jurists. Their association with positive law made them open to the necessities of government, but their reception of moral doctrines justified the high opinion they had of their position and placed them midway between the philosopher and the practitioner.[9] Despite this acknowledgment, Mesnard remained in the mode of political philosopher and never looked beyond constitutional law for the legal substructure of the political ideas he presented.

William F. Church's *Constitutional Thought in Sixteenth-Century France: A Study in the Evolution of Ideas* is a masterful study and is particularly relevant here because the legal basis is broader. He placed more emphasis on the medieval legal traditions. In his sections on Dumoulin and feudal law and on Guy Coquille and customary law, he expanded the terms of the political discussion beyond that of his predecessors. His work is particularly useful for this reason, but it remains, as he presumably intended, in the institutional mode.

One of the earliest works which is still of great value is Georges Weill's 1891 *Les théories sur le pouvoir royal en France pendant les guerres de religion.* He emphasized that much political theory supporting royal power was developed by political and legal writers to justify what was already established in practice. This was done in terms of the king's rights through the Salic law and as God's representative on earth. The new religious beliefs of Luther and Calvin presented a danger to the civil government of France's "Most Christian King."[10] Weill saw that the principle of popular

---

[7] Ibid., 309–348.
[8] Ibid., 491.
[9] Ibid., 15.
[10] Weill, 1–3.

sovereignty, revived from Roman and medieval manifestations during the sixteenth century, was opposed to the royalist doctrine. Monarchical rights, religious rights, and popular rights were the great theories of the time.

According to Weill, the political writers of the sixteenth century did not wish to be innovators, but instead claimed to return to the ancient customs of their ancestors. He discussed the authors according to their various schools of thought, ranging from pure absolutism to limited monarchy. He claimed that there was no real question of a republic in sixteenth-century France. France was sincerely royalist: the question was whether the monarchy should be absolute or limited.[11] All agreed that the fundamental laws limited the monarchy, others believed that the Estates General, Parlement, the princes of the blood, or provincial and local liberties also limited the monarchy's power.[12]

Vittorio de Caprariis's *Propaganda e pensiero politico in Francia durante le guerre di religione* approached the topic of political theory with the perspective of propaganda and political polemic. The subjects and writers discussed are largely the same as in other works, but the elements of pamphlet literature and propaganda bring a new dimension. The first part clarifies the connection between Calvinist political theory and the Huguenot political polemic, and traces the ideas to the development of a political theory of religious toleration. Caprariis brought out the political purpose, as well as the political theory, of L'Hospital, Hotman, Pasquier, Du Haillan, Jean Bodin, and a variety of Huguenot and politique writers.

Caprariis marked an early stage in the study of propaganda for this period. Miriam Yardeni's *La conscience nationale en France pendant les guerres de religion (1559–1598)*[13] is a later work which went beyond him and dealt more extensively with the pamphlet literature as propaganda, particularly as it formed and reflected national consciousness during a period of crisis. Yardeni also noted a major problem with the pamphlet literature: trying to determine to what extent it directed public opinion and to what extent it reflected public opinion. This problem became the focus of many pamphlet studies and was dealt with in an exemplary way in Robert Kingdon's *Myths about the St. Bartholomew's Day Massa-*

---

[11]Ibid., 276–278, 289–290.

[12]Ibid., 278–286.

[13]Miriam Yardeni, *La conscience nationale en France pendant les guerres de religion (1559–1598)* (Louvain: Editions Nauwelaerts, 1971).

cres, 1572–1576.[14] Kingdon's work examines the major (and many minor) pamphlets from this very active period, determines authorship, purpose, and audience for each, and brings to the reader an awareness that these works and their authors had important practical goals beyond the expression of political theory or religious belief. The current project in the following pages develops another dimension expressed in this pamphlet literature, the legal one that underlay much of the political theory and religious argument of sixteenth-century France.

Just War Tradition

The just war arguments of the medieval churchmen used by sixteenth-century Protestant and Catholic writers have also been used frequently as background to twentieth-century just war arguments. Much of this literature was published from the 1960s to the 1980s and was motivated by the United States's involvement in Vietnam, but some works achieved a broader focus.[15] The most comprehensive of the latter works are those of James Turner Johnson and Michael Walzer.

Walzer's *Just and Unjust Wars: A Moral Argument with Historical Illustrations* ranges from the Melian massacre in ancient Greece to the My Lai massacre in Vietnam in an attempt to find the meaning of morality in war. He claims that most people want to act, or at least seem to act, morally even in war.[16] The five sections of his work explore the moral reality of war, theories of aggression, war convention (rules of war), dilemmas, and responsibility. For each topic he uses historical examples drawn primarily from the nineteenth and twentieth centuries, with some also from the eighteenth century and ancient history. He essentially ignored the medieval (except for Agincourt) and the early modern periods. The principles he discusses are, however, generally applicable.

Johnson's *Just War Tradition and the Restraint of War—A Moral and Historical Inquiry* is also a work of broad interest and wide

---

[14]Robert M. Kingdon, *Myths about the St. Bartholomew's Day Massacres, 1572–1576* (Cambridge: Harvard University Press, 1988).

[15]Some recent examples include: James Turner Johnson, *Just War Tradition and the Restraint of War—A Moral and Historical Inquiry* (Princeton: Princeton University Press, 1981); Ronald G. Musto, *The Catholic Peace Tradition* (Maryknoll, NY: Orbis, 1986); Frederick R. Struckmeyer, "The 'Just War' and the Right of Self-Defense," *Ethics* 82 (1971): 48–55; Jenny Teichman, *Pacifism and the Just War* (Oxford: Basil Blackwell, Ltd., 1986); Michael Walzer, *Just and Unjust Wars: A Moral Argument with Historical Illustrations* (New York: Basic Books, 1977); Donald A. Wells, "How Much Can the 'Just War' Justify?" *Journal of Philosophy* 66 (1969): 819–829.

[16]Walzer, 20.

range. However, with the exceptions of a lengthy chapter on the Middle Ages (fifty pages) and a much shorter one (eighteen pages) on the "Transition to the Modern Era," it also essentially ignores the early modern period, although his earlier work *Ideology, Reason, and the Limitation of War: Religious and Secular Concepts 1200–1740*[17] provides a fuller discussion. Nevertheless, Johnson saw this period merely as one in which medieval just war theory was remolded for the modern era. He implied that the thought of the period lacks significance in its own right. On the other hand, in his *Ideology* Johnson did attempt to synthesize the isolated scholarship on the secular, religious, moral, and legal thought on the restraint of war. Even there, however, the emphasis is on the Middle Ages and post-1700 periods, with little attention to the sixteenth century.

These works remain excellent discussions of the development and modern importance of the just war tradition. This is also true of two articles by Donald Wells and Frederick Struckmeyer. Wells argued in his 1969 article, "How Much Can 'The Just War' Justify?" that although the medieval discussions of just war may have added to their moral insights and perhaps made the history of war less awful than it has been, modern war robs terms such as "just," "limited," or "proportional" war and "right intention" of their moral significance. Essentially, he said that the "just war" justifies too much, even genocide when applied in the modern context.[18]

On the other hand, Struckmeyer in his 1971 article, "The 'Just War' and the Right of Self-Defense" disagreed with Wells's sweeping conclusions which dismissed the validity of the entire just war concept. Struckmeyer argued that although he agreed with many of Wells's contentions, Wells did not make sufficient distinctions between fighting for self-defense versus fighting for "righteousness." They are two different things, he said, and the latter is no longer moral.[19] Wells also failed to make a clear distinction between offensive and defensive wars, and instead implied that no wars can be morally justified any longer, and he consistently doubted the motives which lead nations to war.[20]

Wells's moral justification for pacifism was no doubt influenced by the murkiness of the United States's involvement in

---

[17]James Turner Johnson, *Ideology, Reason, and the Limitation of War: Religious and Secular Concepts 1200–1740* (Princeton: Princeton University Press, 1975).

[18]Wells, 828–829.

[19]Struckmeyer, 52.

[20]Ibid., 52, 54.

Vietnam. This focus on Vietnam and more recent Cold War and post-Cold War military involvements has caused many modern just war theorists to consider modern relevance and applicability as their primary criteria. This is ahistorical, understandably so, since many of these writers are political scientists or journalists, not historians.

The work which offers the best historical perspective on the just war tradition is Frederick Russell's *The Just War in the Middle Ages*.[21] This work, however, focuses entirely on the medieval period and, although it is excellent on the development of the tradition, it obviously does not include the use of the just war tradition in sixteenth-century France.

Another historically oriented work is Jenny Teichman's *Pacifism and the Just War* which is in some ways more comprehensive than either Johnson's or Walzer's works, although it is considerably shorter. Her focus is on the topics of her title, without an overwhelmingly obvious bias toward the modern. Since she writes from a British perspective, her work is not preoccupied with the Vietnam era. What she does do is present a well-developed philosophical discussion in historical perspective of the arguments concerning pacifism and just war traditions. Unfortunately, given this comprehensive goal and limited length, once again little space is devoted to the sixteenth century.

Even more comprehensive than Teichman, Ronald Musto's *The Catholic Peace Tradition* exhausts its topic within the framework the author has designed. His subject is the Catholic tradition of peace, however, and therefore has little to say about the just war tradition's contribution to sixteenth-century resistance theory in France. His chapters on the sixteenth century focus on Thomas More and Erasmus, and on the missionary activity in the New World. Rabelais and Montaigne also receive consideration, as do such seventeenth-century figures as Pascal and Vitoria, but again, these are not significant in the present study.

Most of the above works clearly did not intend to focus on sixteenth-century France, but they are the ones which have considered the relevant topic of just war. As useful as these works are within their chosen frameworks, they simply do not discuss the ideas of self-defense and defense of property during the French Wars of Religion, the use of these arguments by individuals to defend their religious and political actions, and the importance of

---

[21]Frederick H. Russell, *The Just War in the Middle Ages* (Cambridge: Cambridge University Press, 1975).

these defense arguments to the development of sixteenth-century resistance theory.

Social Violence

In addition to the contexts of political theory and just war tradition, that of social violence itself is important for the understanding of the context in which resistance theory developed. Violence permeated sixteenth-century French society, even without that generated by the Wars of Religion. In his *Iron and Blood* Henry Heller examined the social conflict of the first half of the sixteenth century to understand better the religious and political "chaos" of the civil wars in the second half.[22] He argued that these peasant uprisings were part of a larger pattern of social conflict which marked the entire century and in which the upper class often took the initiative. Heller stated, "Rather than dealing with just a record of popular protest, we are dealing with a history of both resistance and domination."[23] He argued also, however, that there were elements countering class conflict, particularly the continuation of personal and client relationships, which inhibited social conflict within classes, and the religious affiliations, which tended to reinforce ties across class lines. Local allegiance against the state and the fear of foreign war also created vertical ties between classes.[24]

Nevertheless, he emphasized that French society in 1560 was in a state of crisis, divided by class hostility and economic crisis, as well as by religion. In the 1560s much of the French peasantry, both Catholic and Protestant, refused to pay the tithe. According to Heller, religious popular resistance was directed against the established Church and therefore against the existing political, legal, and social order.[25]

The nobility of the sword[26] persisted in practicing private violence as a manifestation of their noble concept of "honor" and to maintain the independence to which they were accustomed.[27]

---

[22]Henry Heller, *Iron and Blood: Civil Wars in Sixteenth-Century France* (Montreal: McGill-Queen's University Press, 1991).

[23]Ibid., 7.

[24]Ibid., 11.

[25]Ibid., 47–57.

[26]The nobility was divided between the older nobility of the sword (which still represented something of a warrior culture) and the newer nobility of the robe (formed by the ennobled families of the juristic bureaucracy).

[27]Kristen B. Neuschel, *Word of Honor: Interpreting Noble Culture in Sixteenth-Century France* (Ithaca: Cornell University Press, 1989), 17–18.

Kristen Neuschel has examined the debate over the existence of the noble client system and presented a clear summary of the historiography of the question.[28] She has also clarified the complexity of nobles' religious lives in relation to their social and political lives and pointed out, "In any case, shared religious convictions did not ensure concert of interests. . . . The overlapping but distinct arenas of nobles' concern—from strictly local power to the goal of influence over the king—stand out clearly even in an analysis of the wars as religious wars."[29] Even the nobility of the sword used legal arguments to justify their acts or prospective acts of violence.[30]

Neuschel acknowledges that the nobility accepted both the right and the responsibility of self-defense, as the number of weapons in their household inventories indicates. Warmaking in the sixteenth century was both a public and a private responsibility for the nobility and it was also an essential prerogative of their status.[31] Neuschel sees in the conduct of the nobles the revelation that belligerence and actual violence were acceptable and expected kinds of behavior and claims that other aspects of their lives also reflected the sense of identity that their proclivity for violence reveals.[32]

One traditional form of noble violence which has been the subject of recent study is the duel. This version of private violence was an essential part of noble life and self-expression, and is discussed in François Billacois's *Duel dans la société française des XVIe-XVIIe siècles: Essai de psychosociologie historique* and Micheline Cuénin's *Le duel sous l'Ancien Régime*.[33] Billacois describes the duel as part of an ancient tradition in the form of judicial duels and individual combat, although the word duel itself was new in the sixteenth century.[34] Dueling ran counter to monarchical and church policy, but this manifestation of noble violence resisted efforts to put an end to it. Neither the early religious denunciations nor Henry III's ordonnance declaring duels an act of *lèse-majesté* seem to have had much effect.[35]

---

[28]Ibid., 2–30.

[29]Ibid., 33.

[30]Ibid., 46–48. Neuschel cited the case of the sire de Morvilliers who defended himself to Catherine de Medicis in 1567.

[31]Ibid., 63–65.

[32]Ibid., 68.

[33]François Billacois, *Duel dans la société française des XVIe -XVIIe siècles: Essai de psychosociologie historique* (Paris: Editions de l'Ecole des hautes études en sciences sociales, 1986); Micheline Cuénin, *Le duel sous l'Ancien Régime* (Paris: Presses de la Renaissance, 1982).

[34]Billacois, 31.

[35]Ibid., 148.

Cuénin, on the other hand, claims that the duel developed late in the sixteenth century in response to peace following the Wars of Religion. During peacetime, nobles (especially nobles of the sword) used the duel to defend their honor and to gain warrior reputations no longer possible through war. Repeated royal attempts from the time of Henry IV to regulate, punish, or outlaw duels met with little success, suggesting the importance to the nobles of this ritual form of violence.[36]

Arlette Jouanna discussed the role of the traditional nobility in her *Le Devoir de révolte* and devoted approximately one half of the work to the period of the Wars of Religion. Among the usual goals of noble revolt for the period, she identified the political purpose of fighting for the "public good" and the "welfare of the kingdom." The nobles claimed to be fighting for the king, not against him. Although this is often seen as a rhetorical device, she argued that it actually bears witness to their recognition of the "king's two bodies" and the absence of any institutionalized methods for expressing political opposition.[37]

Jouanna focused on the declarations and the pamphlet literature produced by the section of the nobility which believed it was their duty to take arms; she identified this group as the nobility of the sword. The two nobilities, the traditional one of the sword and the newer nobility of the robe, often maintained cordial social relations with each other during this period, but they became increasingly separated from each other as the latter gained power in the royal bureaucracy at the expense of the nobility of the sword.[38] The two nobilities saw the existence of their order and their privileges as an essential part of the French "constitution." They believed that an attack on them was an attack on the body politic and a violation of the laws of the realm.[39] All of the texts justifying the taking of arms underline that the authors have been compelled (*contraints*) to have recourse to violence because legal methods are no longer available. Taking arms might have been illegal, but it was justifiable (*légitime*).[40] Jouanna has seen a political resemblance between the movements of the two groups of nobles during the Wars of Religion in that each claimed that their cause was the public good.[41]

---

[36]Cuénin, 87–89.

[37]Arlette Jouanna, *Le Devoir de révolte: La noblesse française et la gestation de l'Etat moderne, 1559–1661* (Paris: Fayard, 1989), 9–10.

[38]Ibid., 98–99, 392.

[39]Ibid., 393.

[40]Ibid., 165.

[41]Ibid., 180.

Further study of social violence, especially in the rural lower classes, has been done notably by Robert Muchembled. His *La Violence au village* uses judicial documents to capture the *mentalité* of the people of the county of Artois from 1400 to 1660.[42] He argues that violence always played a social role in this region as in others. The peasants in particular, who composed three-fourths of the population, lived constantly with violence.[43] Muchembled argues that in the social milieu of Artois, violence was not necessarily a destabilizing force; violence also had social, ritual, and symbolic forms which often created social cohesion. Some of this violence was designed as a regular defense mechanism against fears and perceived dangers, as well as against outsiders.[44] Violence was an integral part of a society which was intensely contentious.[45]

A recent work which has combined the study of social violence and the use of the pamphlet literature is Denis Crouzet's *Les guerriers de Dieu*.[46] Crouzet has returned the emphasis to religion as the inspiration for violence and gives little space to economic and social factors, to the violence of the military campaigns, or to the violence of the nobles in general: "The religious wars were holy wars, perhaps the most extreme of the holy wars."[47] He draws a distinction between Catholic violence and Protestant (essentially Huguenot) violence.[48] Both sides practiced ritual aggression and were greatly affected by the apocalyptic prophecies of the time which contributed to a collective anxiety, but the form of violence was structured by confessional differences. For the Catholics, the destruction of heresy was necessary for salvation in the face of an imminent Last Judgment. Crouzet sees Catholic violence as irrational, resulting from divine "possession."[49] For the Protestants, violence often took the form of iconoclasm and attacks on Catholic clergy. Crouzet interprets this as preparing the world for Christ's return, and sees it as rational.[50] This distinction is particularly interesting, and somewhat suspect, since the legal and constitutional arguments were the same for both sides, although

---

[42]Robert Muchembled, *The Violence au village: sociabilité et comportements populaires en Artois du XVe au XVIIe siècle* (Turnhout, Belgium: Editions Brepols, 1989).

[43]Ibid., 7, 33–35.

[44]Ibid., ch. 2, especially 118–126.

[45]Ibid., 404.

[46]Denis Crouzet, *Les guerriers de Dieu: La violence au temps des troubles de religion (vers 1525–vers 1610)*, 2 vols. (Seyssel: Champ Vallon, 1990).

[47]Ibid., I, 320.

[48]Ibid., *passim*, especially vol. I, ch. 7 and ch. 9.

[49]Ibid., I, 203, 578.

[50]Ibid., I, 625; II, 242–243.

they tended to use them at different times. In addition, such a distinction does not seem to exist between the truly rational group, the tolerant Catholics and Huguenots.

One of Crouzet's main sources was the pamphlet literature which he approached without emphasizing individual authors; his interest was in following themes (especially biblical and apocalyptic ones) and their public role.[51] He included a discussion of just resistance and just war, but his emphasis on the biblical tradition remains in place.[52] The pamphlets are replete with scriptural references, so this approach is certainly valid, however, there are many other themes and arguments present as well, and Crouzet largely ignores them despite his over fifteen hundred pages of text. The legal arguments which are emphasized in the following essay were certainly not the only ones of importance, but they have been largely ignored in this context and are presented here to add another layer to our understanding of the complexity of sixteenth-century France.

Defense and Resistance

The right to defend oneself and one's property came into early conflict with medieval rulers' attempts to maintain public order and the peace of the kingdom, as is shown by the history of the growth of royal justice in the background section of the current study. As the French monarchy asserted its claims to sovereignty, the concept of *lèse-majesté*, or treason,[53] grew, but so did the belief that the king ruled by popular consent for the good of the kingdom, a commitment acknowledged in his coronation oath. By the late sixteenth century, heresy was being seen as a kind of treason and religious arguments which canonists and theologians had developed over several centuries began to play a vital role in

---

[51]Ibid., I, 47.

[52]Ibid., II, 464–474.

[53]I am using 'lèse-majesté' and our English word 'treason' as essentially equivalent here. By the later Middle Ages, *lèse-majesté* was sometimes described as high treason, which suggests a broader definition for the latter, but by the early seventeenth century an increasing number of crimes were being classed as *lèse-majesté*. For the expansion of *lèse-majesté*, see Sarah Hanley, *The 'Lit de Justice' of the Kings of France: Constitutional Ideology in Legend, Ritual, and Discourse* (Princeton: Princeton University Press, 1983), 173–174 (note 16) and 277 (note 66). It is interesting that this expansion of *lèse-majesté* seems to parallel the growth of royal power itself.

The problem is further complicated by the French word 'trahison' which also translates as treason. *Trahison* was usually a broad term and in some interpretations this crime could be committed by anyone against one's own lord, or even against anyone at all; *trahison* against the king was still *lèse-majesté*, however. See S.H. Cuttler, *Law of Treason and Treason Trials in Later Medieval France* (Cambridge: Cambridge University Press, 1975), 2, 21, 238.

the new context of religious warfare. It was the convergence of these various political, legal, and religious elements during the sixteenth-century Wars of Religion which, in the hands of writers trained in those traditions, resulted in the formulation of theories of resistance which asserted the right of the people (variously defined and limited) to defend themselves against "bad" kings. This work explores the legal theories used to justify that development.

BACKGROUND: THE INDIVIDUAL'S RIGHT TO DEFENSE *VERSUS* THE RIGHTS AND DUTIES OF THE CROWN

Medieval Development of the Right to Defense

Both French law and Roman law (recognized as 'written reason' even where it held no legal force) allowed using violence to defend property as well as one's person. The laws carefully regulated and strictly limited such violence. These limitations were related directly to the amount of force used in the attack, the reason for the attack, and alternatives available to the victim. The Roman law maxim *vim vi repellere licet* (force may repel force) formed the basis of the concept of justified defense against violence. Laws and statutes permitted violent defense against aggression because it was generally believed that both natural law and the *jus gentium* (human law) granted the right of self-defense. As Roman law developed and limited justifiable violence, it restricted the legitimate use of violence to certain conditions, particularly *incontinenti* and *moderamen inculpatae tutelae*. *Incontinenti* referred to the immediate reaction to a violent attack on one's person; generally, immediate repulsion of violence was considered legal.[54] On the other hand, repulsion of violence *ex intervallo*, after a delay, was considered a culpable act.

The second condition, *moderamen inculpatae tutelae* or moderation of blameless protection, restricted violence to "reasonable" limits in the defense of person or property. To react with reasonable moderation to a violent attack rendered the reaction blameless.[55] These two concepts of *incontinenti* and *moderamen inculpatae tutelae* developed within the Roman law to confine private violence to purely defensive acts and thus eliminate vengeance and private wars.

The medieval Roman law scholars adopted these limitations and usually invoked the two concepts of immediacy and moder-

---

[54]*Digest* 43.16.3.9; Frederick H. Russell, *The Just War in the Middle Ages* (Cambridge: Cambridge University Press, 1975), 41–43.

[55]*Code* 8.4.1. Individuals observing the moderation appropriate to the situation can legally defend their rightful possessions against attack. Russell, 41–43.

15

ation together in discussions of self-defense.[56] As medieval law
developed, the concept of using force to repel force spread from
simple self-defense cases into the area of property defense. In the
fourteenth century the jurist Bartolus of Sassoferrato (1313–1357),
commenting on the Roman law codified under Justinian in the
sixth century, argued that thieves could be killed if that was the
only way to protect life or property.[57] He justified killing even
when the threat made was only to property; his main concern
was the recovery of the (movable) property and he based his argument on the principle of force repelling force. If, however, one
recognized the thief and could thus recover the property later,
killing to recover property at the time of the theft was not justifiable. Killing was justified only when the thief was unrecogniz-
able, since in that case later recovery of the property would be
unlikely.[58] Some fourteenth- and fifteenth-century authors continued to use the question of recovery of the property as a main
criterion for justifying violence against thieves. By the sixteenth
century, a new element emerged, and writers concerned themselves with the value of the property in question. They began to
relate value to violence and attempted to determine how valuable
property had to be before one could kill to defend it.[59]

The Norman 'cas ducaux' and the French 'cas royaux'

Many developments in French law occurred first in Normandy
and only later in France proper. The idea that strict protection of
possession was an essential part of public order came to Normandy soon after the middle of the twelfth century, by which
time the duke of Normandy had become the sole effective guard-
ian of the public peace in the duchy.[60]

---

[56]Russell, 41–44, cites Placentinus, *Summa Codicis* to Cod. 8.4 (Mainz, 1536), 374; Azo, *Summa Codicis* to Cod. 8.4 (Lyons, 1564), fols. 215va, 215vb, 216va, and *Summa Codicis* to Cod. 9.12, fol. 239ra. For Innocent IV's expansion of this latter opinion, see Russell, chapter 5, notes 59, 136. Azo, *Lectura in Codicem* to Cod. 8.4.6 (Paris, 1611), 616.

[57]In these discussions of killing to recover property, that in question is movable and cor-poral, which again emphasizes that the right to kill in defense of property was related to the possibility of recovery by other methods. Movable goods could be taken away and hid-den and become unrecoverable. Immovable goods could be recovered in time even if at first the thief could not be identified. For a full discussion, see Shaun J. Sullivan, O.F.M., *Killing in Defense of Private Property: The Development of a Roman Catholic Moral Teaching, Thir-teenth to Eighteenth Centuries* (Missoula, Montana: Scholars Press, 1976), 156.

[58]Ibid., 96–97.

[59]Ibid., 127.

[60]Ernest Perrot, *Les cas royaux: origine et développement de la théorie aux XIIIe et XIVe siècles* (1910; rp., Geneva: Slatkine-Megariotis, 1975), 306–307.

The roots of the movement to *cas ducaux*, or cases reserved to the duke, are connected to the duties imposed on the duke at the time of his coronation. Under the influence of the Church, which tried to give a sacred character to royalty by unction, the duke's coronation oath began to include a clause in which he swore to maintain the peace for all his subjects.[61] The duke, as defender of the peace, took over the protection of *seisin* (possession) and the Assize of 1166 put *disseisin* (dispossession) within the jurisdiction of his court.[62] The possessory procedure of novel disseisin, used in France and England as well as in Normandy, allowed a quick means for landholders to recover possession of property when they believed that they had been illegally ejected from it.[63] It was called "novel" disseisin because to use the procedure the ejectment had to have occurred recently, usually defined as within "a year and a day" of the suit. Such disseisins were rather common in the Middle Ages, sometimes as a result of pure theft, more often as the result of a very real dispute about property rights. When the court heard a case of novel disseisin, it could decide to reinstate a dispossessed holder immediately, thus forcing the disseisor to go through a lengthier legal procedure to establish a legal claim to the property.

Norman possessory procedure eventually combined novel disseisin (recent dispossession) with the more ancient procedure of the crying of *haro*.[64] Novel disseisin and *haro* were both intended to give quick relief. The cry of *haro* developed as an institution of Norman criminal law directed toward making an arrest at the scene of the crime; in civil law, *haro* regulated debates which demanded an urgent solution. The procedure of *haro* had a long evolution. At first it was only an exclamation uttered by the victim or by the witnesses of a flagrant delict, with the intention of calling neighbors to help and publicizing the measure of force which the malefactor compelled them to employ. In this form the institution of *haro* existed in many countries. By the thirteenth century the Norman dukes had added their personal touch. They

---

[61]Ibid., 306–308 for a discussion of the ducal oath.

[62]Ibid., 315 cites ch. 53 of the Norman *Tres Ancien coutume*.

[63]For novel disseisin in Normandy and France, see Perrot, *Les cas royaux* and Joseph R. Strayer, "The Writ of Novel Disseisin in Normandy at the End of the Thirteenth Century," in Joseph R. Strayer, *Medieval Statecraft and the Perspectives of History* (Princeton: Princeton University Press, 1971); for England, see Donald W. Sutherland, *The Assize of Novel Disseisin* (Oxford: Clarendon Press, 1973).

[64]Hippolyte Pissard, *La clameur de haro dans le droit normand* (Caen: L. Jouan, 1911), 95–101.

revived and restored *haro* by regularizing its usage and by ordering their officers to intervene whenever it was used.[65]

The addition to novel disseisin of *haro*, which had become an appeal to the duke for protection, speeded up possessory procedure by stopping any act of disturbing possession.[66] The cry of *haro* became a procedure utilized any time one wished to produce a rapid and conclusive result. It became applicable even to the outlaw or prisoner trying only to escape and who did no damage or injury. Thus, *haro* became styled the *clamor de patriae*, the general appeal addressed by a Norman to other Normans when the "peace of the people" was at stake.[67]

In spite of the extension of the application of *haro*, a vassal could never cry *haro* against his lord, nor a subject against his king. In these cases of pressing peril, the plaintiff could only address a *requête* (a formal request for justice) to the judge. This limitation of *haro* applied especially in matters of taxation. Several ordinances prohibited raising the *haro* against those charged with collecting taxes and denied sergeants, bailiffs, and judges participation in the procedure. Even though *haro* could not be raised against the ducal or royal officers in the normal exercise of their duties, it did become valuable against the magistrates and sergeants who manifestly exceeded the limits of their jurisdiction or abused their power, and against those who committed real frauds. The Norman jurists claimed that these people ought to be treated as "larrons" (robbers).[68]

In France *haro* developed so that one who cried it came under the safeguard of the king.[69] The royal safeguard effectively rendered the royal officers competent to punish outrages committed against the person who was under royal protection.[70] The kings of France, following the Norman lead, came to consider themselves guardians of the public order and considered a breach of public order a blow to themselves.[71] Initially, however, the Crown had little means to enforce its claims as a defender of the public order because this task fell outside the king's recognized rights. By the end of the twelfth century, the king's rights had multiplied

---

[65]Pissard, *La clameur de haro*, 3. For examples of *clameur de haro* see Ernest Perrot, *Arresta communia Scacarii, deux collections d'arrêts notables de l'Echiquier de Normandie* (Caen: L. Jouan, 1910), nos. 80 and 112.

[66]Strayer, 6.

[67]Pissard, *La clameur de haro*, 28.

[68]Ibid., 118–119.

[69]Ibid., 46, cites the *Coutume, stille et usage*, ch. XXI.

[70]Ibid., 46.

[71]Perrot, *Les cas royaux*, 317.

and he had created *baillis* to administer his justice away from the court. These factors led to the creation of the theory of the *cas royaux*, cases reserved to the king as *cas ducaux* were reserved to the duke. As the king's rights became more numerous and better defended during the thirteenth century, the number of cases involving them increased rapidly.

Initially the king did not assume the protection of public peace as part of his interpretation of his social role. Rather than looking for occasions for intervention or taking advantage of sudden disturbances in public order, the king carefully reserved to himself only those cases which touched him personally.[72] This becomes clear in cases of counterfeiting. A number of people besides the king had the right to mint their own coins, but counterfeiting was a *cas royal* only when royal coins were counterfeited. Counterfeiting ducal coins, for example, did not touch the king personally and therefore those cases were not *cas royaux*. If the Crown had considered its intervention in public order as the basis for the *cas royaux*, the seriousness of the delict (murder, arson, rape, and even violent dispossession) should have constituted sufficient reason for making it a *cas royal*. Even though the Crown often avoided conceding these serious cases with the rest of the justice in communal charters, it did not claim them as *cas royaux*. The *cas royaux* sometimes could be quite serious, as in *lèse-majesté;* or constitute a much lighter injury, as in a breach of royal protection; or be more civil than criminal, as in the patrimonial cases of the king.[73]

A discussion of the evolution of the three delicts of *port d'armes* (carrying unauthorized weapons), breach of royal protection, and novel disseisin, all of which involved violence, will help clarify the extent of royal involvement and the royal interpretation of what "touched" the king. The delicts of *port d'armes* and the breach of royal protection became *cas royaux* while novel disseisin, despite the use of violence and threat to peace, never did. The determining feature in each delict was injury (actual or perceived) to the king or to his royal power.

The delict of *port d'armes* became a *cas royal* in the Midi from around 1270 and in the north from the end of the reign of Philip IV (1285–1314).[74] According to the thirteenth-century French jurist Philippe de Beaumanoir (1250–1296), the simple act of moving about in an armed group constituted a punishable offense. If

---

[72]Ibid., 321–322.
[73]Ibid.
[74]Perrot, *Les cas royaux*, 263–265.

such armed men committed a crime, they answered to the king or to the baron for the delict of *port d'armes*, and to the local seigneurial justice for the *crime ordinaire*.[75] It seems reasonable that the royal justices often knew of the violence committed by individuals assembled in arms. In an effort to clarify the juridical theory, when the delicts were easily separable the royal justices retained jurisdiction only in that which troubled the king.[76]

Ernest Perrot concluded that the evolution of the delict of *port d'armes* into a *cas royal* probably came about as a result of the necessities of political order rather than for any purely judicial reason. Private warfare had become so widespread that seigneurial justices could no longer control it. A superior power had to impose order, especially since the very nobles who controlled seigneurial justice were the most frequent violators of the public order. The king must have discovered rapidly that he alone, by his position of sovereignty and by his own force, could impose his will on the lords. This purely practical utility led to the development of the delict of *port d'armes* into a *cas royal*.[77]

In the case of the breach of royal protection, the king was considered to have been touched by the act which violated the protection. Consequently, if this delict was flagrant it was removed to royal jurisdiction from the local judge's jurisdiction or, if the case were ordinary, it was removed to royal jurisdiction from the competence of the judge of the domicile of the delinquent. The victim was allowed to exercise his revenge through the medium of royal justice. But if the act violating the protection seemed serious enough to constitute an attack on the public order, according to the custom of the place, there could be a second delict in addition to the *cas royal*, and a second prosecution by the seigneurial judge.[78]

One would think that *novel disseisin* would have developed rapidly into a *cas royal*. This is true especially since every novel disseisin involved violence, or at least a manifest disturbance of the peace, and the king now had become the recognized keeper of

---

[75]Philippe de Remi, sire de Beaumanoir, *Coutumes de Beauvaisis*, A. Salmon, ed. (Paris: A. Picard et fils, 1899–1900), vol. 2, ch. 58, no. 1654: "Se aucun vont par mi autrui justice a force et a armes, et il font en cell justice aucun mesfet et el i sont pris et aresté par celui a qui la justice apartient, il doit avoir l'amende et la justice du mesfait; et il rois ou cil qui tient en baronie, se ce fu fet en sa baronie, doit avoir l'amende des armes; car s'il passassent outre armé sans mesfere, si fussent il en l'amende des armes porter, si qu'il doivent l'amende du mesfet et l'amende des armes porter seur la defense le roi. . . ."

[76]Perrot, *Les cas royaux*, 291–292.

[77]Ibid., 263–265.

[78]Ibid., 292–294.

the public peace. He alone was competent to stop the state of things unjustly created by violence or by fraud.[79] Novel disseisin, however, remained only a *cas de prévention absolue*[80] and did not become a *cas royal*. The *arrêts* emanating from the Parlement of Paris which settled the difficulties of jurisdiction relevant to novel disseisins all related to the *cas de prévention*. The king decided that in general the jurisdiction ought to remain with the seigneurs, and that if the charge of novel disseisin were proposed against the lord by one of his vassals, the case went to the lord's court. A case which had no feudal connection could not return to the seigneurial judge, however, and became simply a *cas de prévention absolue*. Throughout the fourteenth century, legal writers saw disseisin as a *cas de prévention* and in spite of the fact that *port d'armes* had become a *cas royal*, they made no such claim for novel disseisin. Even the royal documents considered possessory actions only as the *cas de simple prévention absolue*. As late as the sixteenth and seventeenth centuries, authors generally, though no longer unanimously, claimed that novel disseisin was not a case reserved to the royal justices alone.[81] Novel disseisin had its own character, however, and in some ways tended to be thought of as a *cas royal* even if it was not declared such.

'Lèse-Majesté' and Confiscation

The development of the *cas royaux* seems to have been part of the thirteenth-century developments in which sovereign states emerged as their own judges concerning the necessity of self-defense. The Roman law was adapted to make the king "emperor in his own kingdom." Around 1284 Beaumanoir ascribed to the French king the power required to defend his own kingdom.[82] He also went so far as to claim that "each baron was sovereign in his own barony," and that the count of Clermont had special rights over his subjects' property in wartime because of his concern for the common good.[83] Beaumanoir, however, restricted the right of the barons to wage war. While they could fight their own wars,

---

[79]Ibid., 188–189.

[80]The *cas de prévention absolue* was a case in a seigneurial court in which the king maintained the right of peremptory intervention if he did not consider the seigneur's justice sufficiently expeditious. Such cases were removed to the jurisdiction of the royal courts on an individual basis.

[81]This discussion is based on Perrot, *Les cas royaux*, 201–203.

[82]Beaumanoir, vol. 2, ch. 49, no. 1510.

[83]Ibid., ch. 34, no. 1043; ch. 58, no. 1662.

he claimed they were prohibited from waging war against their king or resisting his justice.[84] His middle position of allowing some private war but also recognizing the centralized royal justice reflected the real situation in northern France at the time of his writing. According to Frederick Russell, "It was just this shifting mosaic of conflicting jurisdiction upon which Innocent IV based his distinction between the just war and defense. Only later did royal jurisdiction develop into full sovereignty."[85]

Subjects owed loyalty to their king under divine, human, and feudal law. In medieval France *lèse-majesté* was the greatest of crimes since it was an injury against public authority as represented by the king. *Lèse-majesté* was the worst crime one could commit against the king or the "state," as heresy was the worst sin recognized by the Church.

The French law of treason[86] developed from the Roman law concept of *laesa maiestas*, which gave the monarchy a legal justification for its attempts to maintain public order and quell political crises. Charges against the Crown of arbitrary repression or of personal vengeance could be answered with counter-charges of *lèse-majesté*, or treason.[87] The treason laws were necessarily based on *lèse-majesté* rather than on the more feudal foundation of the breach of a sworn oath of fidelity because, in a strict sense, infidelity was only an unwarranted breach of faith. The oath of fidelity simply represented a voluntary joint contract of vassalage which allowed a wronged vassal the right to seek justice against his lord through formal defiance or rebellion. This source of law placed the vassal in a position from which he could conduct a valid war of defense for his legitimate rights and, for this reason, it was not a suitable choice for the basis of any royal law of treason.[88]

Those crimes which usurped or disregarded the king's sovereignty had begun to constitute treason or *lèse-majesté* in medieval France, following the lead of ducal Normandy. Such acts as the

---

[84]Ibid., ch. 59, no. 1673; Cf. Maurice Keen, *The Laws of War in the Late Middle Ages* (London: Routledge and K. Paul, 1965), 73ff.

[85]Russell, 300–301.

[86]See above, note 53.

[87]S.H. Cuttler, *Law of Treason and Treason Trials in Later Medieval France* (Cambridge: Cambridge University Press, 1981), 238.

[88]Ibid., 5. See also Richard W. Kaeuper, *War, Justice, and Public Order: England and France in the Later Middle Ages* (New York: Oxford University Press, 1988), 230–231. According to Kaeuper, war against the Crown developed gradually into treason in France in the early fourteenth century. Rebellious nobles under the last Capetians were seldom charged with treason, but the Valois Philip VI executed rebels for treason and confiscated their property. The Valois also used treason charges against urban uprisings.

illicit convocation of assemblies, negotiation of independent
agreements with the enemy, secret communication with the enemy, and even the violation of the king's safeguard, eventually
constituted treasonous offenses since they affronted the king's
honor, majesty, and authority.[89]

As the royal authority increasingly included the duties of maintaining both public order and private rights, the Crown ran into
jurisdictional conflicts with its feudal vassals. In the case of forfeiture of property for treason, the Crown's claims conflicted with
claims of feudal lords and those who held rights of high justice in
their own territories.[90] Such property had a political importance
since it could be used for political patronage as well as profit.

Eventually, any act which "injured the king, the royal line, or
the kingdom, or that otherwise diminished the authority of the
Crown—or was intended to do so—was treason."[91] By developing a broad definition of treason, the Crown could maintain public order more easily since the treason law made punishment
readily available to it. By declaring certain behavior treasonous,
the Crown could extend royal power against other jurisdictions
and since punishment for treason included confiscation of movable and immovable property, the Crown benefited both politically and financially.[92]

Since lands confiscated by the king could be granted freely at
his will, they could be used as rewards to his loyal followers, as
support for his relatives, or they could be returned all or in part
to the traitor or, more likely, to the traitor's heirs.[93] Evidence for
the reversal of these judgments appears in the collections of royal
laws for the fifteenth and sixteenth centuries and indicates the
usefulness of this technique to royal authority.[94] By using confiscated property wisely, the king could reward loyalty at little expense to himself and maintain some control, especially over the

---

[89]Cuttler, 44–45.

[90]Ibid., 1–3 and P.-C. Timbal, "La confiscation dans le droit français des XIIIe et XIVe siècles," *Revue historique de droit français et étranger* 4th ser. 22 (1943): 70 and 4th ser. 22 (1944): 36–37, 41.

[91]Cuttler, 54.

[92]Ibid., 54, 121; 94–95 for confiscation by the king of lands of the peers; 116 for capital punishment and lesser penalties such as fines. See also F.-A. Isambert, ed., *Recueil général des anciennes lois françaises. Depuis l'an 420 jusqu'à la révolution de 1789* (Paris, 1822–1833), vol. 12, pp. 590–591, no. 285, *Edit portant confiscation au profit du roi des biens de ceux qui seront condamnés comme criminels de lèse-majesté, et portant que la confiscation s'étendra tant sur les biens personnels du condamné que sur les fiefs inférieurs et sur les meubles, nonobstant toutes substitutions,* 10 August 1539; and vol. 12, p. 694, no. 314, *Déclaration relative à la confiscation prononcée contre les criminels de lèse majesté,* 13 November 1540.

[93]Cuttler, 125–131 and 134–136; Timbal, vol. 22 (1944): 43–44; 59–60.

[94]For some of these cases, see below, note 150.

nobility, by the threat and action of confiscation and the possibility of its reversal.

Popular Consent and the Coronation Oath

The idea of popular sovereignty had become increasingly common with the medieval revival of Roman law. Writers commenting on the Roman civil law interpreted the *lex regia* passages of Justinian's *Digest* as meaning that the emperor's or king's authority originally came from the people. There was some doubt as to whether and when the Roman people had transferred their power to the emperor,[95] and the issue of the election of the French kings also raised questions. According to Richard Jackson, sixteenth-century theorists developed two basic positions: they felt either kingship had been elective but was no longer so, or they denied that kingship had ever been elective.[96] There was generally agreement, however, that any practice of electing French kings had been abolished by the time of the Capetians, if not before. For most of the writers believing in a historic practice of election, the remnants of election remained in the ceremonies of coronation and consecration.[97]

The sixteenth-century coronation ceremony contained a *consensus populi* (consent of the people, popular consent) which most likely resulted from a conflation of older elements.[98] The suggestion of election at the ceremony was quickly applied by proponents of the theories of resistance, and Théodore de Bèze went so far as to imply in his 1574 *Du droit des magistrats (Right of Magistrates)* that the kingship still could be elective, and he reminded his readers that even in his day the French kings still took an oath at their anointment.[99] In the 1579 *Vindiciae contra tyrannos (Judgment Against Tyrants)*, which Jackson has described as the "most highly developed theory of elective kingship which the Huguenots put forth,"[100] the pseudonymous author Etienne Junius Bru-

---

[95]For example, Etienne Pasquier did not believe that the Roman people had ever transferred their power to the emperor. He could find no mention of such a law and believed that Ulpian had invented it to flatter his master, the emperor Alexander. See Etienne Pasquier, *L'interprétation des Institutes de Justinian* (Paris, 1847; rp. Geneva: Slatkine Reprints, 1970), Livre I, Ch. 10, 25–26.

[96]Richard A. Jackson, "Elective Kingship and *Consensus Populi* in Sixteenth-Century France," *Journal of Modern History* 44 (June 1972): 164.

[97]Ibid., *passim* and Jean B. Brissaud, *A History of French Public Law* (South Hackensack, New Jersey: Rothman Reprints, 1969), 341.

[98]Jackson, 159.

[99]Théodore de Bèze, *Du droit des magistrats*, ed. Robert M. Kingdon (Geneva: Librairie Droz, 1970), 42, 44.

[100]Jackson, 160.

tus (probably Philippe Duplessis-Mornay, but also attributed to Hubert Languet) claimed that a twofold covenant was made at the coronation: the first part among God, the king, and the people; and the second between the king and the people. The latter stipulated that the people would obey the king if he were a proper ruler.[101] François Hotman's *Francogallia* (appearing initially in 1573 after the St. Bartholomew's Day massacres, but begun earlier) first clearly laid out the claim for royal election, but Hotman admitted that in France in his time kings succeeded by "force of custom."[102]

Jean Bodin chose to ignore the evidence for an election in favor of the coronation oath itself, and he argued that the *consensus populi* represented a confirmation of the ceremony of coronation rather than a true form of election.[103] Pierre de Belloy, in his *Apologie catholique* (published in 1585 after the excommunication of Henry of Navarre) argued that the anointment and consecration were actually unnecessary to the coronation and served largely as a public declaration of the king, thus countering the arguments of those who claimed that the Huguenot Henry of Navarre could never be king of France because he could not be "consecrated, anointed and crowned according to the ancient custom."[104] He further argued that the kingship was primarily successive and the coronation ceremony was simply a mark of honor.[105]

From another viewpoint, the question was not one of elective elements in the coronation oath, but of contractual elements. The feudal contract, as any contract, carried rights and duties for all parties. This concept of mutual obligation permeated the complaints from all sides in the religious wars. The idea of popular sovereignty itself depended in part on this idea of feudal contract.[106]

Proponents of these ideas of contract and popular sovereignty based their arguments on reason and on ideas of contract from

---

[101]*Vindiciae contra tyrannos*, French trans. of 1581, ed. A. Jouanna, *et al.* (Geneva: Librairie Droz, 1979), 25–26.

[102]François Hotman, *Francogallia*, variorum edition; Latin text by Ralph E. Giesey, translated by J.H.M. Salmon (Cambridge: Cambridge University Press, 1972), 220–233 and 464–467.

[103]Jean Bodin, *Six Books of a Commonweale*, trans. by Richard Knolles, 1606 (Cambridge: Harvard University Press, 1962), Book 6, Ch. 5, 731–732.

[104]Pierre de Belloy, (Also attributed to Edmond de Lalouette), *Apologie Catholiqve contre les libelles declarations, advis, et consvltations faictes, escrites, & publiees par les Liguez Perturbateurs du repos du Royaume de France: qui se sont esleuez depuis le deces de feu Monseigneur frere vnique du Roy* (n.p., 1585), fol. 44v.

[105]Ibid., fols. 13v-19r; 43v-44v.

[106]Donald R. Kelley, *The Beginning of Ideology: Consciousness and Society in the French Reformation* (Cambridge: Cambridge University Press, 1981), 317–318.

private law. As a contract between a king and his people, the coronation oath bound both parties. The king had to observe the oath unless the people released him from it or the equity of the law he had sworn to keep ceased to run.[107] In this feudal view of kingship, royalty was not absolute. The Crown was not truly hereditary since the king actually was neither the heir of his predecessor nor his successor in personal property, but the royal successor through the law of blood, the Salic law. Put simply, this meant that the king could neither change nor establish royal succession by his own testament.[108] In the same way, permanent transfer of jurisdiction was impossible when the rights belonged exclusively to the Crown.[109]

The essence of royalty was the king's supreme lordship over the territories of his kingdom,[110] but he was not the owner of the kingdom and therefore could not alienate nor abdicate his lordship. He was only the administrator, *non censetur dominus seu proprietarius regni sui, sed administrator.*[111] The king's rights in his kingdom resembled those that a husband had in his wife's dowry. They were a collection of legal rights involving fictional ownership and true inalienability. Dumoulin summarized this royal administrative role: *Imò etiam supremus princeps non est fundatus in dominio rerum particularium, nec dicitur universalis dominus nisi quoad jurisdictionem et protectionem.*[112] The king could not alienate the royal domain because it belonged to the Crown, not to him.[113]

In his coronation oath the king swore to obey the law, defend the faith and protect his subjects and their property. The inclu-

---

[107]J.H.M. Salmon, *The French Religious Wars in English Political Thought* (Oxford: Clarendon Press, 1959), 47–48.

[108]Gert Meyer, "Charles Dumoulin. Ein führender französischer Rechts Gelehrter," *Rechts-und sozial wissenschaftliche Vorträge und Schriften,* 4 (Nuremburg, 1956), 42–43. See also Ralph E. Giesey, "The Juristic Basis of the Dynastic Right to the French Throne," *Transactions of the American Philosophical Society* 51, pt. 5 (1961): especially 12–22. The latter work is under revision.

[109]Meyer, 43, cites Charles Dumoulin, *Traité de fiefs,* sec. 3, gl. 13, no. 10: "Nullus alius potest habere dominium alicuius jurisdictionis seu jurisdictionem jure et nomine proprio, nisi solum de iure speciali ex investitura et concessione regis mediata vel immediata," and *Traité de fiefs,* sec. 3, gl. 4, no. 18 and sec. 1, gl. 3, no. 28: "Iurisdictio de se est inabdicabilis a rege, moliente rege nec est separabilis a regia dignitate. . . . Non potest rex abdicare totam administrationem iurisdictionis seu potestatis regiae, etiam quoad aliquem locum vel aliquam personam regni."

[110]M.H. Aubépin, *De l'influence de Dumoulin sur la législation française* (Paris: Libraire du conseil d'Etat, vol. 1, 1855), 8–9, cites Dumoulin, *Traité de fiefs,* sec. 3, gl. 4, no. 15.

[111]Ibid., cites *Traité de fiefs,* sec. 3, gl. 4, no. 17.

[112]Ibid., cites *Traité de fiefs,* sec. 67, gl. 2, no. 5.

[113]Meyers, 43, cites Dumoulin, *Traité de fiefs,* sec.43, gl. 1, no. 184: ". . . cuius proprietas spectat ad maiestatem et coronam et non ad personam organicam principis," and *Traité de fiefs,* sec. 1, gl. 5, nos. 53–56. For the development of the images of the king's relation to his kingdom as a marriage and of the domain as a dowry, see Hanley, *The 'Lit de Justice',* 77–79, 83–84, 86, 95–99.

sion of his duty to defend the faith obligated him to fight heresy. This could often be assumed under his duties to maintain order as well, since most people saw active heresy as a threat to the peace of the kingdom. In addition, since the king was supposed to protect the faith, any challenge to that faith became a kind of treason.

The Church and Confiscation for Heresy

Since heresy could be seen as *lèse-majesté*, it is not surprising that forfeiture and confiscation were usual punishment for convicted heretics. There were canon law (church law) precedents for this action as well.

The canonists had legitimated the holy war against the Saracens, pagans, and other "infidels." These legal writers of the Church also taught that certain circumstances allowed for the preaching of holy wars against heretical and unorthodox Christians, and Causa 23 in Gratian's *Decretum* supported this idea. This passage was based on a case of heretics forcing their beliefs on the faithful, and Gratian cited authorities supporting the use of force by the Church to suppress heresy.[114] He considered the use of force legitimate when employed against "wicked" persons.[115]

Gratian's *Decretum* formed the starting point for the thirteenth-century development of the doctrine of the right to war. Two main groups contributed to this development: the canonists, inspired to elaborate the Roman and canon laws; and the theologians, notably Saint Thomas Aquinas, inspired in part by the principles of Saint Augustine.[116] The canonists wrote detailed commentaries on special cases and paid special attention to problems of property and restitution. The theologians, on the other hand, held more directly to fundamental principles, seeking motivation and justification for the right to war and the use of war as

---

[114]*Corpus Juris Canonici Gregorii XIII* (Graz: Akademische druck-u verlagsanstalt, 1959), vol. 1, *Decretum Magistri Gratiani*, C. 23 q. 3 c. 3; C. 23 q.4 c. 48. Causa 23, questio 3, c. 3: "Catholici aduersus hereticos a potestatibus ordinatus defensionem postulare possunt. Item Augustinus ad Emeritum, (epist. CLXIV). Nostri aduersus illicitas et priuatas uestrorum uiolentias (quas et uos ibi, qui talia facitis, doletis et gemitis) a potestatibus ordinatis ultionem petunt, non quod hos persequantur, sed quia se defendant. (col. 897). But see also *Decretum* C. 28, q. 1, c. 11 "Iudaeorum" for his opposition to forced baptism of Jews and a discussion of a sixteenth-century debate on this subject in Steven Rowan, "Ulrich Zasius and the Baptism of Jewish Children," *Sixteenth Century Journal* 6 (October 1973): 3–25 and Rowan, "Ulrich Zasius and John Eck: 'Faith need not be kept with an enemy,' " *Sixteenth Century Journal* 8 (Summer 1977): 79–95.

[115]*Decretum*, C. 23 q. 5 d.p.c. 48; C. 23 q. 6 pr. and d.p.c. 4.

[116]Robert Regout, *La doctrine de la guerre juste de Saint Augustin à nos jours* (Paris: A. Pedone, 1935), 67.

vindictive justice. Neither view was isolated: the canonists also
dealt with punitive war and the theologians thought defense and
restitution of property were so obvious that they had to go beyond them.[117]

The Decretists (canonists writing on Gratian's *Decretum*) had
denied heretics the protection of the human law because the heretics' false beliefs violated divine law and canon law and because
heretics persecuted the Church. Rolandus (who became Pope Alexander III, 1159–1181) claimed that heretics lost all their rights to
property; Huguccio (d. 1210) claimed that princes had an obligation to defend the Church against heretics and schismatics, and
that this should be done by making war on them.[118] Since they
had no rights under law, heretics had no legal claim to property,
which therefore could be confiscated in a just war. Under the
same principle, heretics could not justly possess Church property
and orthodox Christians could take possession when acting on
proper authority. Huguccio (who taught Lotharius of Segni who
later became Pope Innocent III) justified war against heretics because they offended God by their unbelief and unjustly held
property legitimately belonging to Christians under divine law.
He interpreted divine law as giving the pious a right to expel the
impious and to retain possession of territory they captured without sinful intentions.[119] This created a great potential for
possessory actions on the part of those disseised in such cases.
Huguccio's attacks on the rights of even peaceful non-Christians
became a justification for the Crusades to the Holy Land to expel
the Saracens from land which many Christians believed belonged
to them by a divine religious right.[120] It is not surprising that the
invasion of the Crusades resulted in a defensive response, which
was essentially a "just war."

How the Church would apply the crusade closer to home became clear rather quickly during the early thirteenth century in
the attack on the Albigensians in Languedoc. When Peter of Ara-
gon (1196–1213) and Philip Augustus (1180–1223), the sovereigns
of the Midi's heretical princes, refused to suppress their heretic
vassals and confiscate their fiefs, the papacy became interested
in organizing the army directed against the Albigensians and
promised spiritual and temporal benefits to those faithful who

---

[117]Ibid., 141.
[118]James A. Brundage, "The Holy War and Medieval Lawyers," in Thomas Patrick Murphy, *The Holy War* (Columbus: Ohio State University Press, 1976), 122–123.
[119]Russell, 113–115.
[120]Ibid.

enlisted.[121] In a letter of March 1208, Innocent III (1198–1216) appealed directly to the barons of France, ignoring their sovereign Philip Augustus. They agreed to go to combat, under the direction of the papal legate. The Church took charge of the expedition, substituting itself in the role of authority usually belonging to the temporal power.[122]

The papacy asserted its prerogative to carry out hostilities against heretical vassals and to confiscate their goods in spite of the opposition of the sovereign; it confined itself to reserving the homage and the services due to the latter. Innocent III, however, died almost immediately after the Fourth Lateran Council promulgated this doctrine in 1215. The secular powers, now represented by the new French king Louis VIII (1223–1226), became more closely interested in the crusade and in the recovery of the lost territory. The new king claimed for himself the initiative of the crusade, directing operations and collaborating with the pope through his legate.[123] Since Louis VIII, who was also sovereign of Languedoc, now accepted an active role against the heretics, the Church needed to fulfill only its spiritual role. The Church pronounced religious penalties against the heretics, called down on them the vengeance of civil power, absolved the guilty, set their penance, and supervised the fulfillment of the crusaders' vows. The king conducted the war, proscribed heretics, and confiscated their goods.[124]

The Fourth Lateran Council, meeting in 1215, had decided that it was within the power of the pope to take all measures necessary for the extinction of heresy and to sequester a contaminated territory. The goal of the "holy war" was the extermination of heretics and in this the Church believed that it could not be regulated. Heretics were outside the law and could not claim its protection. The Church or the secular sovereign acted against them as justices with absolute power and not as they would have acted against a common adversary.

The Decretalists (canonists writing on the papal letters, or decretals) adopted the Roman law dictum that violence could be repelled by violence (*vim vi repellere licet*). Based on this and their

---

[121]Hippolyte Pissard, *La Guerre Sainte en pays chrétien; essai sur l'origine et le développement des théories canoniques* (Paris: A. Picard et fils, 1912), 44.

[122]Ibid., 40–41; Michel Villey, *La croisade: Essai sur la formation d'une théorie juridique* (Paris: Vrin, 1942), 221. Following the papal legate may not have seemed so strange to the barons. Earlier, during Louis VII's absence on crusade from 1147–1149, the entire kingdom had been under the Church's protection and was essentially governed by Abbot Suger. See Kaeuper, *War, Justice, and Public Order*, 149.

[123]Pissard, *La Guerre Sainte*, 63.

[124]Ibid., 74–75.

interpretations of the decretals, they reinterpreted Gratian's phrase, *iusta bella ulciscuntur iniurias* and drew a distinction between the repulsion of injuries or the recovery of goods unjustly seized by persons under orders from their prince, and similar actions performed by persons acting without proper authority or cases of unjust punishment; the latter actions were condemned.[125]

Joannes Teutonicus (d. 1245 or 1246), in his *Glossa ordinaria* on Gratian's *Decretum* developed this differentiation into a general theory of licit repulsion of violence. He recognized vengeful motives only if the person attacked sought to strike an adversary after the immediate danger had passed. Prior to that one was considered to be justly defending oneself. *Iniuria* became assimilated to *violentia* and either could be repelled *incontinenti* as long as the defense was moderate. A person had the right to repel violence with violence if he or his property was attacked.[126] To this Raymond of Peñafort (c.1180–1275) added the restriction that anyone who went beyond the limitations of moderation in his defense deserved excommunication because he was acting out of vengeance. He added a further limitation concerning the defense of property when he declared that anyone wounding or killing an attacker while expelling him from his property also deserved excommunication.[127]

Even though Hostiensis (c.1200–1271) and Raymond of Peñafort both supported the use of violence in defense and knew that Roman and canon law accepted it, they had suspicions about the rights of private persons to do the same. Raymond's idea of not fighting back at all as a way of aspiring to perfection was not practical and found few followers. Hostiensis later argued from Roman and canon law that it was licit to injure one's attackers in repelling them and that repulsion of violence by violence *incontinenti* was not to be considered vengeful.[128] All violent acts, except immediate self-defense, required the approval of a superior authority.[129] This limitation removed some of the suspicions concerning private persons' use of violence. The Decretalists used Roman law to develop a theory of just war in which the ideas of justice and legality became closely assimilated. Russell described

---

[125]Russell, 131.

[126]Ibid., 132. Russell says that Joannes Teutonicus skillfully combined Decretist and Romanistic analyses in this interpretation.

[127]Ibid., 131–132.

[128]Ibid.

[129]Ibid., 297–298; Regout, 69.

this as the development of war as an "extraordinary form of a lawsuit."[130]

Before people could have a legal right to defend property violently, they had to have the right to hold property, whether movable or immovable. Hostiensis believed that non-Christians, or "infidels," had no right at all to possess property[131] and that war between the faithful and unfaithful was always a just war for the faithful. Pope Innocent IV (1243–1254) refuted this opinion of Hostiensis in the *Apparatus ad Decretalia*, cap. *de vota*, claiming that it was not permissible to invade territory occupied by infidels simply because they were infidels. He reasoned that God had created everything and so the earth and all of its inhabitants belonged to him. In the beginning God had exercised all power himself; later he allowed men to rule. For these reasons, sovereignty, property, and jurisdiction could undoubtedly exist among the unfaithful, as God's gift. Therefore, the pope had no more right to take from the unfaithful than he did to take from the faithful.[132] Hostiensis criticized Innocent IV for his devotion to Roman law in general as well as on this particular issue.

Saint Thomas Aquinas (1225–1274) also concluded that being non-Christian did not hinder one's ability to own property or to rule. He argued that the right to hold property came from either the natural law or the human law and a person does not lose it by infidelity. He also pointed out that both Saint Paul and Saint Peter ordered the people to obey princes who were all infidels, and they told the slaves to obey their masters.[133] Therefore, he concluded, it is forbidden to seize property from Saracens, Jews, or other unfaithful. To take their property was as much theft as was taking property from a fellow Christian.[134] This religious toleration suggested by Innocent IV and Aquinas did not receive general acceptance for centuries, and confiscation became a central issue in sixteenth-century French discussions of heresy. On the other hand, this same tradition generally held that property could be taken rightfully in war, if the war was just.

The just war tradition (which formed a basis for the justification of crusades and religious wars) was gleaned from Saint Augustine, put in legal terms by Gratian in the twelfth century, and

---

[130]Russell, 297.
[131]Alfred Vanderpol, *La doctrine scolastique du droit de guerre* (Paris, A. Pedone, 1925), 225.
[132]Ibid., 226–227.
[133]Ibid., 228.
[134]Ibid.

clarified scholastically by Aquinas in the thirteenth century. Aquinas's theory of right to war (*jus ad bellum*) is found mainly in four short articles in his *Summa Theologica*. The first of these articles is the most important; the other three deal successively with the participation of clerks in combat, stratagems of war, and the pursuit of hostilities on public holidays.[135] Aquinas took his inspiration entirely from Augustine, especially from his texts assembled in Gratian's *Decretum*. He did not mention the ideas of Raymond, Hostiensis, or Innocent IV on war, although their works had been known for twenty years.[136] Aquinas listed three conditions necessary for a just war: the authority of a prince on whose order the war is made; a just cause, that is to say, the enemy deserves to be fought by reason of a fault; and the right intention of the belligerents, who must be fighting for the repression of evil, not for revenge.[137]

Although authorities can trace the Christian theory of just war to Augustinian and Thomistic roots, in fact there was no real just war doctrine in either Augustine or the medieval theologians or canonists. The classic form of the doctrine, including both the right to make war (*jus ad bellum*) and the restrictions on what was allowable in war in terms of fighting methods (*jus in bello*) which make up what is now considered a complete just war doctrine, did not truly exist in the Middle Ages because the theory was split into separate doctrines: the canonical one of rights to war and the secular one of rights in war.[138]

Between the time of Aquinas and the sixteenth- and seventeenth-century commentators, the doctrine of *jus ad bellum* had also developed in two directions. To the older approach which made a just war primarily an assertion of God's judgment against evildoers was added the description of a just war as the assertion of a prince's right to retaliate against troublers of his own domains.[139] In discussing the emergence of religion as a type of legitimation for war in the sixteenth century, Konrad Repgen claimed:

War and the use of military force against heterodoxy was a right assumed by all four of the great churches. War, however, was no longer

---

[135]Regout, 80.

[136]Ibid.

[137]Ibid., 81.

[138]James Turner Johnson, *Ideology, Reason, and the Limitation of War: Religious and Secular Concepts 1200–1740* (Princeton: Princeton University Press, 1975), 7–8.

[139]Ibid., 55.

waged *and* justified as a crusade but as *Religionskrieg,* as the military solution to conflicts arising from the protection of confessional possessions or from confessional conquest.[140]

Contributing factors in the development of secular religious war
came from the acceptance of the idea that the prince's power
came from the community below, or from some part of it, rather
than solely from God above. The prince could act in the name of
the people as well as in the name of God.[141]

Confiscation for Treason and Heresy in France[142]

With the numerous canon law precedents justifying the use of
force against heretics and the confiscation of their property, and
the Norman and French precedents for royal protection of peace
and property, the French developed their own legal support for
the confiscation of the property of heretics in the royal edict of
1535.[143] An added provision, which allowed a quarter of the
property to go to the informers, made the edict particularly odi-
ous to many.[144]

Those families which suffered as a result of this policy in the
sixteenth century tended to develop a strong religious hatred and
a desire for revenge.[145] Property was seen as an extension of self;
the nobility of the family was closely tied to land and inheritance.[146] Furthermore, property was not only land, but the rights

---

[140]Konrad Repgen, "What is 'Religious War'?" in E.I. Kouri and Tom Scott, *Politics and Society in Reformation Europe: Essays for Sir Geoffrey Elton on His Sixty-fifth Birthday* (New York: Macmillan, 1987), 323. Emphasis is Repgen's. His analysis focuses specifically on issues and arguments at the beginning of the Schmalkaldic war in 1546 but intentionally draws wider implications for sixteenth-century warfare.

[141]Johnson, 55.

[142]The material in this section appeared previously in slightly different form in my ar-
ticle "Neither Treason nor Heresy: Use of Defense Arguments to Avoid Forfeiture during the French Wars of Religion," *The Sixteenth Century Journal* 22 (Winter 1991): 705–716.

[143]Isambert, vol. 12, pp. 402–403, no. 211, *Edit portant que les receleurs de lutheriens seront punis des mêmes peines qu'eux s'ils ne les livrent à la justice; et que les dénonciateurs auront le quart des confiscations,* Paris, 29 January 1534; registered by the Parlement of Paris on 1 February. [Since they began the new year with Easter, the year is actually 1535 in modern dating.]

[144]See Jean Sambuc, "Documents sur la réforme dans le Comtat et en Provence," *Bulletin de la Société de l'histoire du protestantisme française,* 117 (1971): 629–636.

[145]Marie Camille Alfred, Vicomte de Meaux, *Les luttes religieuses en France au seizième siècle* (Paris: E. Plon et Cie, 1879), 48–49.

[146]J.R. Hale, *War and Society in Renaissance Europe, 1450–1620* (Baltimore: Johns Hopkins University Press, 1985), 22. Hale's remarks apply particularly to the nobility of the sword, but family and inheritance were also a major concern of the nobility of the robe as well. See Sarah Hanley, "Engendering the State: Family Formation and State Building in Early Modern France," *French Historical Studies* 16 (Spring 1989): 4–27.

attached to the land and this formed a vital part of family identity over time.[147] To forfeit the family property, especially for such horrible crimes as heresy and treason, meant the death of the family if the heirs could not achieve restitution of the estate.[148] P.-C. Timbal stated that the early writers actually justified confiscation on the grounds that having such a severe penalty fall on criminals' descendants would deter them from committing these crimes in the first place.[149]

The frequency of restoration in cases of treason shows the Crown's recognition of the value of leniency towards the heirs, if not towards the traitors themselves.[150] The Crown usually did not wish to destroy whole noble families and lines by enforcing a permanent forfeiture. Heresy was a different, more emotional issue, however, and often involved the entire family. In a society in which status was based largely on land ownership and title to office, losing the family estate was a greater threat to the continuation of the family than the death of an individual member and did not carry the same heavenly reward as martyrdom.[151]

It is not surprising then that the Huguenots in France attempted to avoid charges that their religious doctrines carried

---

[147]Neuschel, 147.

[148]In the English law Bracton had made attainder for treason the most solemn penalty: it resulted not only in brutal corporal punishments and the forfeiture of all possessions, but in the legal death of the family. See Henry de Bracton, *De Legibus et Consuetudinibus Angliae*, G.E. Woodbine, ed. (New Haven: Yale University Press, 1915–1942), vol. 2, 335 on the heinousness of treason; and J.R. Lander, "Attainder and Forfeiture 1453–1509," *Historical Journal* 4 (1961): 119. Feudal opinion largely opposed this severity and entailed estates were generally protected from forfeiture for treason (Lander, 119.)

[149]Timbal, vol. 22 (1944): 53–54.

[150]For relevant cases in which confiscations were reversed, see the entries pertaining to Jacques Coeur in Isambert, *Recueil général*, vol. 9, pp. 254–256, no. 214, *Arrêt d'une commission présidée par le roi, qui condamne J. Coeur, lui fait grâce de la vie, et confisque ses biens*, 19 May 1453; vol. 9, pp. 361–363, no. 248, *Lettres d'abolition en faveur de ceux qui n'ont pas révélé à la justice les biens de Jacques Coeur*, 11 May 1459; vol. 9, pp. 469–472, no. 55, *Lettres qui mettent Geoffroi Coeur en possession des terres et domaines confisqués sur Jacques Coeur son père*, August 1463. For other cases, see *Ordonnances des roys de France de la troisième race: recueillies par ordre chronologique*, ed. E.-J. de Laurière *et al.* (Paris: Imprimerie royale, 1723–1849), vol. 19, pp. 458–461, 28 January 1484 a)*Lettres pour comprendre au Traité d'Arras* b)*Jacques de Savoie* c)*Marie de Luxembourg sa femme* d)*et Françoise soeur de Marie; Restitution ordonnée des Biens confisqués sur leur aïeul*. In these cases the king ordering restitution was the successor to one who had confiscated the property and the restitution was made to the heirs of the felons. Cuttler, 134–141, also includes a number of cases of full or partial restitution, especially Jacques Coeur, Charles de Melun, Louis de Luxembourg, Jean d'Armagnac and Jacques d'Armagnac.

[151]For a discussion of the importance of the martyr concept (or complex) to Protestants in this period, see Donald R. Kelley, "Martyrs, Myths, and the Massacre: the Background of St. Bartholomew," *American Historical Review* 77 (December 1972): 1323–1342 and Robert M. Kingdon, *Myths about the St. Bartholomew's Day Massacres, 1572–1576* (Cambridge: Harvard University Press, 1988), especially ch. 2.

subversive elements. The threats of death and confiscation for either treason or heresy were very real ones, even in the reigns of Francis I and Henry II, before the religious civil wars actually began.[152] When Huguenot and other anti-Guisard writers decided that armed resistance was necessary in the 1560s, they openly declared that the war was not directed against the king, but against the Duke of Guise and his followers. They justified this war on the grounds that the Guise brothers were traitors and tyrants who had usurped the royal power. This approach to the problem is shown clearly in passages from the contemporary political pamphlets which refer to the Guise family as "Tyrants" in one case,[153] and in another charge them with usurping authority and illegal administration, and accuse them of "hoping by this method to authorize a tyranny under the title of a just principality."[154] The authors pleaded with the princes of the blood to save France from the tyranny of the Guises' control of the regency of Francis II. They said that the people had been oppressed by the "tyranny and cruelty of the House of Guise, which has seized the person of the King and the power of France, partly by force, partly by shrewdness. . . ."[155]

These pleas for deliverance from the tyranny of the evil counselors have a nice medieval sound, complicated by the king himself being a minor. Those willing to take arms defended themselves in print against the charges of rebelling against their king: "When one speaks of a rebel, one lays that incontinently on us, as if we would not wish to obey the King. . . ."[156] The so-called rebels did not see themselves as rebels or trai-

---

[152]Carlos M.N. Eire, *War against the Idols: The Reformation of Worship from Erasmus to Calvin* (New York: Cambridge University Press, 1986), 235–236 and 283 for persecution of Protestants under Francis I, Henry II, and Francis II. See also Kelley, "Martyrs, Myths, and the Massacre," 1329–1330.

[153]*Response av livre inscrit povr la maiorité dv Roy Francois II*, 1560 in *Mémoires de Condé, ou Recueil pour servir à l'histoire de France. Contenant ce qui s'est passé de plus memorable sans ce Royaume sous les Regnes de François II et Charles IX* (London: Claude du Bosse; J. Nillor et Cies, 1740), tome 1, 193.

[154]*Legitime conseil des Roys de France pendant leur iuvne aage, Contre ceux qui veulent maintenir l'illegitime gouuernement de ceux de Guise, soubz le tiltre de la Maiorité du Roy . . .* , 1560?: "Esperans par ce moyen d'authoriser vne tyrannie, soubs le tiltre d'une iuste principauté." in *Mémoires de Condé*, tome 1, 225–226.

[155]*Svpplication et Remonstrance addressee av Roy de Navarre & autres Princes du Sang de France, pour la deliurance du Roy & du Royaume*, 1560?: ". . . qui de longtemps se sentent oppressez de la tyrannie & cruauté de la maison de Guise qui s'est saisie de la force, personne du Roy & emparee de la puissance de la France, partie par force partie par finess,. . ." in *Mémoires de Condé*, tome 1, 257.

[156]*Remonstrance a tovs estats. Par laquelle est en brief demonstré la foy & innocence des vrays Chrestiens*, 1561?: "Quand on parle d'vn rebelle, l'on met incontinent cela sur nous, comme si nous ne voulions obeir au Roy. . ." in *Mémoires de Condé*, tome 2, 850–851.

tors, but as defenders of the monarchy, saviors of the king and of France.[157]

The sixteenth-century activists recognized the necessity of remaining within the prescribed limits of the law when advocating or using violence. The ethical and practical issues which they faced paralleled those which Roman law writers had raised concerning self-defense and canonists and theologians had raised while developing the arguments for just war. Those who opposed the king during the sixteenth century often sought to avoid legal condemnation by claiming self-defense when their violence became the basis of court action. When the issue was forced to the battlefield, the opposition had to justify the taking of arms.

First the Huguenots in 1562 and then the Catholics in 1576 justified arming themselves against the king's will with the argument that they were not taking arms against the authority of the king, but against heresy and evil counselors of the king. They did this in defense of themselves, their property, their king, and their religion. Both sides repeated these arguments at different times as their political strengths varied. They appealed to the king as the proper authority to maintain order and to fight heresy. Contemporaries often based these appeals on the king's legal duties and obligations under the coronation oath: his promises to obey the law, defend the faith, and protect his subjects and their property. There was also a similarity in the ideology of resistance between radical Catholics and Huguenots when they made their revolutionary appeals. Quentin Skinner has shown the extent to which Calvinist revolutionary thought was influenced by late medieval legal and political thought and concluded:

Once we see, however, how little of their [the Huguenots'] ideology is distinctively Calvinist, we are bound to ask whether they may have been concerned not only with efforts at self-definition, but also with ap-

---

[157] A parallel can be drawn here between those who claimed their resistance to the Guise family was justified to save the monarchy and the fifteenth-century claims of justifiable tyrannicide made by Jean Petit for the Duke of Burgundy, Jean Sans Peur, who had assassinated Charles VI's brother Louis d'Orléans. In the latter case, the king's life was seen to be in danger from his brother, and the assassination was a preventive measure to save the king. The Duke of Burgundy's actions were defended by Jean Petit in his *Justification du duc de Bourgogne*, which claimed that the assassins of Louis d'Orléans had acted for the good of the king and of the kingdom. (Although both François Hotman in his *Francogallia* and Jean Boucher in his *De iusta Henri Tertii: Abdicatione e francorum* discuss other cases of tyrannicide, neither mentions this one.) For a complete discussion see Alfred Coville, *Jean Petit: La question du tyrannicide au commencement du XVe siècle* (Paris, 1932; Rp. Geneva: Slatkine Reprints, 1974), especially 455–456 for the specific propositions put forth by Jean Petit.

pealing to the uncommitted, seeking to reassure those who might be thinking of joining the cause, and above all attempting to neutralize as far as possible the hostile Catholic majority by showing them the extent to which revolutionary political actions could be legitimated in terms of impeccably Catholic beliefs.[158]

---

[158]Quentin Skinner, "The Origins of the Calvinist Theory of Revolution," in *After the Reformation: Essays in Honor of J.H. Hexter,* ed. Barbara C. Malament (Philadelphia: University of Pennsylvania Press, 1980), 325.

DEFENSE AND THE RIGHT TO RESIST

Since a king's obligation to protect his people and defend the true religion was sworn to in his coronation oath, a breach of that responsibility could, according to some theorists, justify correction of a ruler by the lesser magistrates.[159] The personal responsibility of the magistrates for their own actions as well as for those of the king seems to have been widely accepted during the sixteenth century, although earlier medieval theorists (such as Marsilius of Padua and John of Salisbury) had not named any representative group as having such responsibility. Sovereignty could easily be conflated with power since sovereignty in the abstract could be associated either with the personal authority of the king or with the magistrates who could act for or against the king in the name of the community.[160]

As in medieval theory, a just war could be levied only on the proper authority of a ruler, so once rebels lost their fight, the king could treat them as traitors rather than as honorably defeated enemies. In the royalist interpretation only the king could properly represent public authority. If the disagreement between the king and his opponents did not come to open warfare, however, the affront to the king's authority remained an indirect one, a private dispute which threatened the king largely as a disruption of public order. This type of war came more under the old feudal concept of a breach of a sworn oath and to be legitimate had to meet certain criteria necessary for such an interpretation. S.H. Cuttler lists these criteria as: the necessity for the dispute to be a lawful one, the prior existence of a denial of justice, and the limitation of the physical combat to the parties directly involved.[161]

Catherine de Medici, acting for her minor son Charles IX, evoked the argument of the "good of the kingdom" many times, notably in the edicts of pacification and to justify religious toler-

---

[159]A magistrate is a civil official with the power to administer the law. In sixteenth-century France this included aristocrats and members of the city governments, such as mayors and members of councils, as well as officials of the central government.

[160]Salmon, *The French Religious Wars*, 40.

[161]Cuttler, 32. See also Keen, 109.

ation, especially before 1568.[162] The numerous edicts of pacification issued in the sixteenth century had as their goal the creation of a general peace in the realm which would enable all the king's subjects to return to business as usual. None of these attempts quite succeeded. None of the pleas for toleration in this period seem to have been based on the arguments of Pope Innocent IV and Thomas Aquinas that religious belief did not affect the right to hold property. Part of the reason for the continued unrest under the edicts of pacification lay in the radical Catholic determination to destroy heresy and achieve religious concord, by violence if necessary.[163] The edicts were seen by the radical Catholics as a sign of weakness in the monarchy.

Even before the St. Bartholomew's Day massacres in 1572 the Huguenots viewed the Catholic determination to uproot them as an illegal attack justifying a violent self-defense and claimed their fight had always been in self-defense against persecution, or for the rights of the princes of the blood to control the regency, but certainly not in opposition to the king. They had always supported the monarchy, especially when others tried to usurp its powers. This is not surprising since, as a minority in the kingdom, the Huguenots had previously found royal protection the most certain guarantee against persecution.

With the Crown's early failure to support the extreme Catholic cause, supporters began to place their confidence in the House of Guise as the standard-bearer of French Catholicism. For this reason the first phase of the Huguenot resistance in the 1560s was directed against the Guise family and other advisors of the king, not the king himself or the monarchy. These opposition forces sought to legitimate their movement by claiming the leadership of some princes of the blood, as they stated in the *Traicte D'Association faicte par Mon-Seigneur le Prince de Condé auec les Princes, Cheualiers de l'ordre, Seigneurs, Capitaines, Gentils-hommes, & autres* . . . in 1562.[164] Again in a letter of 7 April 1562, Condé

---

[162]For example, the *Edit de Janvier de 1562* in *Mémoires de Condé*, tome 3, 1–11; also in French Political Pamphlets in the Newberry Library. [Listed in Robert O. Lindsay and John Neu, *French Political Pamphlets 1547–1648: A Catalogue of Major Collections in American Libraries* (Madison: University of Wisconsin Press, 1969), no. 284.]

[163]For a discussion of the alternation of policy between concord (unity) and tolerance, see Mario Turchetti, "Religious Concord and Political Tolerance in Sixteenth- and Seventeenth-Century France," *Sixteenth Century Journal* 22 (Spring 1991): 15–25.

[164]*Traicte D'Association faicte par Mon-Seigneur le Prince de Condé auec les Princes, Cheualiers de l'ordre, Seigneurs, Capitaines, Gentils-hommes, & autres . . . pour maintenir l'honneur de Dieu, le repos de ce Royaume, & l'estat & liberté du Roy, sous le gouuernement de la Royne sa mere,* 1562, in French Political Pamphlets in the Newberry Library (Listed in Lindsay and Neu, no. 271).

wrote that they must resist the "violence and efforts of the enemies of the Christian religion who hold our King and the Queen
captives. . ." and they must stop them from carrying out their
designs which would lead only to "the ruin of the faithful and
consequently of this kingdom. . . ."[165]

Catholic claims that the Protestants were rebels against the
king, heretics, and responsible for the disturbances in the kingdom necessitated these defensive statements. Pamphlets such as
the 1560 *Catholique Remonstrance aux Roys et Princes Chrestiens . . .
touchant l'abolition des heresies, troubles & scismes qui regnent auiour-
d'huy en la Chrestienté* had claimed that heresy was the most dangerous crime in the kingdom.[166] By 1562 the charges had become
more explicit and so had the punishments. According to an *arrêt*
of the Parlement, all those who had "taken arms against the
King, pillaged and sacked the Churches . . . are declared Rebels
and criminals of *lèse-majesté*, divine and human, public enemies
of God, of the Crown of France, and disturbers of the repose
and tranquility of the King's subjects."[167] As was to be expected
in cases of *lèse-majesté*, their property was to be confiscated for
the king.[168]

The Huguenots and Condé could defend themselves against
these charges only by further protests that the charges were false
and that the Huguenots, despite this judgment against them
by the Parlement of Paris, armed themselves for the service of
the king, the conservation of the authority of the Estates, and
to resist the violence and tyranny of the Guise faction; they
had no intention of rebelling against their king.[169] The need
to be armed came as a result of the violence directed against

---

[165]*Lettre de Monsieur le Prince de Condé, avx églises reformees de France*, 1562, in *Mémoires de
Condé*, tome 3, 172: ". . . de resister aux violences & efforts que les ennemis de la Religion
Chrestienne & qui tiennent nostre Roy & la Royne captifs, . . . & executer leurs desseings,
qui ne tendent qu'a la ruine des fideles & consequement de ce Royaume. . . ."

[166]*Catholique Remonstrance aux Roys et Princes Chrestiens . . . touchant l'abolition des heresies,
troubles & scismes qui regnent auiourd'huy en la Chrestienté*, 1560 French trans. of Latin text by
M. Iean de la Vacquerie, in French Political Pamphlets in the Newberry Library (Lindsay
and Neu, no. 212).

[167]*L'Arrest de la court de Parlement publié le dernier iour de Iuin dernier passé, touchant les Rebelles, & perturbateurs du repos & tranquillité des subiects du Roy*, Paris 1562, in French Political
Pamphlets in the Newberry Library (Lindsay and Neu, no. 277): "Dit, que tous ceulx qui
se trouueront auoir pris les armes contre le Roy, pillé & saccagé les Eglises . . . sont de-
clarez & les declare Rebelles & crimineux de lese Maiesté diuine & humaine au premier
chef, ennemis publics de Dieu, de la couronne de France, & perturbateurs du repos &
tranquillité des subiects du Roy."

[168]Ibid.

[169]*Remonstrance de Monseignevr le Prince de Condé et ses associez à la Royne, Sur le iugement
de rebellion donné contre eux par leurs ennemis, se disans estre la Cour de Parlement de Paris, . . .*
in *Mémoires de Condé*, tome 3, 404–427; 405: ". . . on pretend declarer rebelles ceux qui se
sont armez pour le seruice du Roy, la conseruation de l'authorité des Estats, & pour resister à la violence & tyrannie des sieurs de Guyse & leurs adherans. . . ."

them which took the forms of murder, pillaging, assaults on women, and "other horrible excesses" even after the publication of the edicts of pacification.[170] It was the king's sworn duty to protect his subjects. If he did not do it, they did it themselves, in his name.

When the Huguenots fought in 1567 they succeeded in recovering some of the ground they had lost politically. It was this improved situation, however, which in part led to the St. Bartholomew's Day massacres. The weak monarchy, under a regency during the 1560s, had been willing to compromise with the Protestants to preserve peace. It was against this early policy of toleration that the first leagues had been formed by local Catholic nobles and prelates. The improvement in the Protestant position annoyed many Catholics and disconcerted the papacy. Pius V had urged Charles IX to seek total annihilation of the "heresy."[171] The St. Bartholomew's Day massacres were an attempt to put the policy into effect.

Following St. Bartholomew's Day, the massacres of Protestants went beyond the capital and into the provinces where "Huguenot-hunting" became something of a sport.[172] This was possible, despite early confusion over the cause and motivation of the massacres, because the king (Charles IX) had taken his own stand against the Huguenots when he announced that he had ordered the massacre in Paris. The king himself declared that what happened on 24 August had been done at his express order to prevent the implementation of a hateful conspiracy by Admiral Coligny and his accomplices against the king and his Estate.[173] Heresy had clearly become treason and just war theory became increasingly secularized as it developed into resistance theory.

---

[170]*Remonstrance envoyee au Roy, par la noblesse de la Religion reformee du Païs et Conté du Maine*, presented to the king at Roussillon 10 August 1564, in *Mémoires de Condé*, tome 6, 327–366 and *Advertissement des crimes horribles, commis par les Seditieux Catoliques Romains, Au Pays & Conté du Maine, Depuis le mois de Iuillet 1564, iusques au mois d'Auril 1565*, in *Mémoires de Condé*, tome 6, 367–407.

[171]See Laderchi, *Annales ecclesiastici*, tom. XXII, anno 1567, 378–391, sec. 7–28; tom. XXIII, anno 1568, 125–218, cited in Meaux, *Luttes religieuses*, 136–137.

[172]Kelley, "Martyrs, Myths, and the Massacre," 1338 (citing François Hotman). See also Philip Benedict, "The Saint Bartholomew's Massacres in the Provinces," *The Historical Journal* 21 (June 1978): 205–225.

[173]Isambert, vol. 14, part 1, pp. 257–259, no. 175, *Déclaration par laquelle la roi se reconnaît l'auteur du massacre de la Saint-Barthélemy*, 28 August 1572. Also in *Declaration du Roy de la cause et occasion de la mort de l'Admiral, & autres ses adherens & complices dernierement advenue en ceste ville de Paris le xxiiii, jour de present mois d'Aoust*, Paris 1572, in French Political Pamphlets in the Newberry Library (Lindsay and Neu, no. 729).

For the early reasons and explanations of the massacres, see Robert M. Kingdon, *Myths about the St. Bartholomew's Day Massacres, 1572–1576* (Cambridge: Harvard University Press, 1988), especially 34–55, 100–101. See also James R. Smither, "The St. Bartholomew's Day Massacre and Images of Kingship in France, 1572–1574," *The Sixteenth Century Journal* 22 (Spring 1991): 27–46.

As the Huguenots began to feel the loss of support by the monarchy itself, they based their arguments on a form of historical constitutionalism founded in a mythical past and supported by claims of immemorial custom.[174] The massacres in 1572 forced Huguenot theorists into a new position. They continued to use the constitutional and historical arguments and the legal precedents, but now these had become something of a mask for more truly revolutionary ideals. They used the new arguments to reason that true sovereignty belonged to the community and enabled its representatives to discipline, depose, or even assassinate the ruler.[175] In this way, Hotman reminded his readers that the Parlement of Paris had to approve the king's laws and edicts before they had any force,[176] and Bèze claimed that it was the duty of the lesser magistrates to resist tyranny and safeguard the people until the Estates, or whoever held the legislative power of the kingdom, could provide for the public welfare.[177] Bèze went further and claimed that the Estates had the authority to appoint and to depose the chief officers of the Crown, or at least to supervise the king in doing so.[178] Arguing from the law of fiefs, Bèze declared that since a lord lost his fief for committing a felony against his vassal, a king must also lose his fief, or kingdom, for committing a felony against his subjects.[179] This feudal basis for forfeiture of the kingdom was repeated in the *Vindiciae contra tyrannos* and tied to the covenant made at the coronation ceremony.[180] The author of the *Vindiciae* took this another step toward legitimate rebellion against a king by declaring that a king who committed a felony against the people also committed *lèse-majesté* against the kingdom and was no better than any other rebel.[181]

---

[174]Salmon, *French Religious Wars*, 6.

[175]For a detailed discussion of the following treatises, see Ralph E. Giesey, "The Monarchomach Triumvirs: Hotman, Beza, and Mornay," *Bibliothèque d'humanisme et renaissance* 32 (January 1970): 41–56 (for the *Francogallia, Du Droit des magistrats*, and the *Vindiciae contra tyrannos*) and Sarah Hanley, "The French Constitution Revised: Representative Assemblies and Resistance Right in the Sixteenth Century" in Mack P. Holt, ed., *Society and Institutions in Renaissance and Early Modern France* (Athens: University of Georgia Press, 1991): 36–50 (for the *Discourses politiques des diverses puissances*), as well as her earlier "The *Discours Politiques* in Monarchomach Ideology: Resistance Right in Sixteenth-Century France," in *Assemblee di Stati e Istituzioni Rappresentative nella Storia del Pensiero Politico Moderno* (Perugia, 1982): 121–134. Kingdon, *Myths*, discusses *Franco-Gallia* in ch. 8, *Du Droit des magistrats* in ch. 9, and *Discours politiques* in ch. 11.

[176]Hotman, *Francogallia*, 458–459.

[177]Bèze, *Du droit des magistrats*, 19, 44.

[178]Ibid., 41–42.

[179]Ibid., 51–52.

[180]*Vindiciae contra tyrannos*, 25–26.

[181]Ibid., 219.

The anonymous *Discours politiques des diverses puissances establies de Dieu au monde* (1574), on the other hand, provided for a legal process to eradicate tyranny and also allowed for assassination. According to the *Discours politiques*, a tyrannical king could be tried and deposed by the "Estates,"[182] but if the king refused to let them meet, he was tacitly assumed to be guilty and automatically deposed.[183] The author justified this action with the argument that sovereignty belongs to the community, whose grant of sovereignty to the king is conditional and who can withdraw the grant if it is abused.[184] If all else fails to remove the tyrant, assassination is permissible.[185]

The St. Bartholomew's Day massacres also stimulated a new exaltation of patriotism and religion on the Catholic side of the debate. As a result, the Huguenots were punished not so much for the supposed heresy, but for their supposed treason. This was made easier since heresy was seen as a kind of treason. The Catholic opposition had never believed the earlier Protestant claims to have been fighting for, rather than against, the king. This becomes clear in their writings which increasingly included such references to the Huguenots as:

those who have for thirteen years often taken arms against the king, and often made attacks against his person and his Estate . . . and try by sharp reasons, and by specious examples to make us believe that their intention was holy and just and that they intended only the increase of the glory of God, to the grandeur and prosperity of the king, and the good and repose of his people and his Kingdom.[186]

The war against these alleged traitors was considered a just one, as the titles alone of some of the pamphlets suggest: *Discovrs svr les occvrrences des gverres intestines de ce Royavme, et de la ivstice de*

---

[182]This is not the Estates General, but a peculiar representative body apparently of the anonymous author's own devising. Hanley calls this the "Assembly of Public Assessors" and notes its similarity to the composition of the *lit de justice* assembly. See Hanley, "French Constitution Revised," 39.

[183]Ibid., 41.

[184]Ibid., 38.

[185]Ibid., 41. According to Kingdon, *Myths*, 181, if the king prevents them from meeting, the leaders of the kingdom should go to war to achieve the same end. This goes beyond Hanley's reading of the text.

[186]*Discovrs Sur les causes de l'execution faite és personnes de ceux qui auoient coniure contre le Roy & son Estat*, Paris 1572, in French Political Pamphlets in the Newberry Library (Lindsay and Neu, no. 723): ". . . ceux qui depuis treize ans ont souuent prins les armes contre le Roy, & souuent attenté contre sa personne & son Estat . . . & voulu par viues raisons, & par exemples captieux nous faire croire que leur intention estoit sainte & iuste, & qu'elle ne tendoit qui à l'augmentation de la gloire de Dieu, à la grandeur & prosperité du Roy, & au bien & repos de son peuple & de son Royaume."

Dieu contre le rebelles au Roy, & comme de droict divin, est licite à sa maiesté punir ses subiets, pour la Religion violée.[187] In the 1573 Edict of Pacification the king again ordered: "all those who during the present war had seized houses, goods, and revenues belonging to Ecclesiastics, or other Catholics, and who held and occupied them, will relinquish to them complete possession and peaceful enjoyment in full liberty and security."[188]

The king's orders did not seem to change the situation for the Catholics, who continued to voice their fears and complaints. In 1574 a number of Catholics complained that conditions were universally bad for them:

The people are not only ruined, but dead, so that of a hundred hearths in one parish, there remain only thirty or forty. And nevertheless, those which remain have been laid waste. Though laid waste, it [the parish] is charged for all such tailles as it ever was, in a manner that to pay these taxes, they have sold almost everything down to the beds, their wives' dresses, some the tiles of their houses, . . . but dare one to say, if there were money in the marrow of their legs, they would have to break their bones to get at it.[189]

The same work carries another complaint of the Catholics, that certain persons, previously without name or title, now have been established in the highest places, have great treasure, and possess the finest houses in France.[190] These complaints did not end, but became more insistent with time. As Henry III showed more favor to the Protestants, Catholic objections went from pleas and advice to the taking of arms in "defense of the monarchy," thus echoing Protestant claims which had begun twenty-five years earlier.

---

[187]Paris 1572, in French Political Pamphlets in the Newberry Library (Lindsay and Neu, no. 724).

[188]*Edict dv Roy svr la Pacification des Troubles de ce Royaume*, 11 August 1573, Paris, 1573, fol. 5r in French Political Pamphlets in the Newberry Library (Lindsay and Neu, no. 755): "Et que tous ceux qui durant la presente guerre se sont emparez des maisons, biens & reuenues appartenans aux Ecclesiastiques, ou autres Catholiques, & qui les tiennent & occupent, leur en delaisseront l'entiere possession & paisible iouissance en toute liberté & seureté."

[189]*Advis et Treshvmbles remonstrances à tous Princes, Seigneurs, Cours de Parlemens & suiets de ce Royaume: par vn bon grand nombre de Catholiques, tant de l'Estat Ecclesiastique, la noblesse que tiers Estat, sur la mauuaise & vniuerselle disposition des afaires*, 1574, in Goulart, *Mémoires de l'Estat de France sous Charles IX*, tome 3, fols. 33v-34: "Le peuple non seulement destruit, mais mort: en sorte que de cent feux en vne paroisse, n'en reste que trente ou quarante: & neantmoins ce qui reste, ruiné qu'il est chargé toutefois de toutes & telles tailles qu'il fut onques: de façon que pour les payer, tous presques on vendu iusques aux licts & robbes de leurs femmes, aucuns la tuille de leurs maisons . . . mais ose lon dire, s'il y a de l'argent en la moelle de leurs iambes, qu'il faut rompres les os pour l'auoir." Also in French Political Pamphlets in the Newberry Library (Lindsay and Neu, no. 776).

[190]Ibid., fol. 32v.

The earliest declarations of the Catholic League in 1576 upheld a constitutional claim to sovereignty for the Estates General of the realm, as well as for the king. This claim was stated specifically in Article II of the Articles of the League drawn up in 1576.[191] Although League theory was not always so clearly stated as in these articles, from the beginning the Leaguers showed their hostility to any theory of monarchy which placed supreme control in the hands of the king.[192] This demand for a somewhat regulated monarchy was not unique to the Leaguer theoreticians, for not only had it been a functional aspect of the medieval monarchy, but Claude de Seyssel had developed it at the beginning of the century and the Huguenot publicists had elaborated it prior to 1572. The weak monarchy, often under a regency during the 1560s and 1570s, was willing to compromise with the Protestants to preserve peace.[193] It was against this early policy of toleration that the first leagues had been formed by Catholic nobles and prelates.

With the Crown's increasing lack of sympathy for the extreme Catholic cause, supporters began to place their confidence in the House of Guise. The Guise family could not really be considered French, although several of the brothers at the time of the Wars of Religion were endowed with French lands and the eldest was connected to the French Crown by marriage. Having French possessions, in addition to their claims in Lorraine, the Guises could and did pose as representatives of the French nobility, claimed rights against the Crown, and maintained claims to the great offices and government posts; as foreigners they could disclaim all responsibilities and duties to the French king and levy war against him while apparently avoiding the charge of lèse-majesté.[194] Their rights and duties concerning the French monarchy had their bases in feudal relationships involving sworn oaths, which did not form a solid basis for charges of lèse-majesté.

The new outbreaks of violence and warfare prompted the writing of treatises on the right and justification for Christians to carry arms or do violence, especially after Henry III ascended the throne. In general these pieces followed the same pattern as medieval ones, and allowed for a moderate use of violence in defending oneself against attack. The author of the pamphlet Traitte

---

[191]The articles of the Catholic League, 1576, are included in P.V. Palma Cayet, Chronologie novenaire in Claude B. Petitot, ed., Collection complète des mémoires relatifs à l'histoire de France, ser. 1, tome 38 (Paris: Foucault, 1825), 254–257.

[192]Allen, 343.

[193]Turchetti, 21–23.

[194]E. Armstrong, The French Wars of Religion: Their Political Aspect (London: Percival and Co., 1904), 47.

Dv Qvel on peʋt apprendre en quel cas il est permis à l'homme Chrestien de porter les armes... cited the *Unde vi* (*Code* 8.4, Whence by violence) of Justinian. This pamphlet appears to be related to the mini-war of pamphlets between "François Portus" and "Pierre Charpentier" (or Carpentier) which Robert Kingdon has discussed.[195] Early in the treatise the author supports a Christian man's right to self-defense: "Let us take the case of a Christian assaulted by brigands in the forest. Is he not permitted at all to defend himself and stop such violence that is done to him, if he keeps to moderation in his defense?" He asks this as a challenge to those who argue otherwise.[196] He then cites the *Unde vi* of the *Code* and extrapolates from the individual to the nation: "If our country is attacked by some enemy, cannot a Christian man oppose such an enemy . . . ?"[197] The author insists that distinctions must be made among types of fighting, since it is clear to him that not all combat is forbidden to Christian men.[198] He divides combat into two categories and claims that it was fighting for revenge that Christ and the Apostles banned, but fighting done by permission on proper authority was approved by them.[199] It would be absurd to think, as the author Fabre claims Charpentier does, that the God permitting the use of arms in the Mosaic Law of the Old Testament was a different God from the one in the Gospels of the New Testament. The same God is the author of both Testaments, and if He allowed wars in the Old Testament to execute his justice, He also approved them for the same cause in the New Testament.[200]

Once the author established the right to carry arms and fight in good conscience, he went on to establish that France was oppressed by tyranny[201] and that the purpose of resistance was not to obtain private vengeance (which would have negated any claim to be fighting either in self-defense or in a just war) but to

---

[195]*Traitte Dv Qvel on peʋt apprendre en quel cas il est permis à l'homme Chrestien de porter les armes et par leqʋel est respondu à Pierre Charpentier, tendant à fin d'empescher la paix, & nous laisser la guerre*, par Pierre Fabre à Monsieur de Lomainie, Baron de Terride, & de Seriniac, trans. from Latin, 1576, 16, in French Political Pamphlets in the Newberry Library (Lindsay and Neu, no. 877). It is not clear exactly where Pierre Charpentier stood in the ongoing debates. See Kingdon, *Myths*, 112–118 for a discussion of Charpentier and of works attributed to him.

[196]*Traitte Dv Qvel on peʋt apprendre*, 15: "Mettons le cas qu'un Chrestien soit assailli par les brigans en vne forest, ne luy est-il point loisible lors de se defendre, & empescher que telle violence ne luy soit faite, gardant toutesfois vne moderation en se defendant?"

[197]Ibid., 16: "Si nostre patrie vient à estre assaillie par quelque ennemi, en ce faict l'homme Chrestien ne peut-il point s'opposer à tel ennemi, & combattre,..?"

[198]Ibid., 16–17.

[199]Ibid., 17.

[200]Ibid., 17–18.

[201]Ibid., 29.

defend the welfare of the kingdom. They carried out this defense of the kingdom not as private men without public authority, but on the authority of the royal edicts and on the authority and power of the three Estates.[202]

The Edict of Pacification of 1576, like that of 1573, demanded the return of Church property from all who had taken it.[203] These same demands were repeated as well in the 1578 Edict of Pacification,[204] but continued violations required further repetitions in the 1579 *Arrest della covrt des grandz Iours seant en la Ville de Poictiers* which threatened those found guilty with penalties of confiscation and being declared attainted,[205] and yet another Edict of Pacification in 1581.[206] Those who continued to violate the edicts of pacification and similar royal prohibitions were seen as rebels and breakers of the peace and would be punished as violators and disturbers of the public peace.[207]

---

[202]Ibid., 29–30.

[203]Isambert, vol. 14, part II, pp. 280–302, no. 46, May 1576, *Edict sur la pacification des troubles du royaume, les protestants, les religionnaires fugitifs, la convocation des Estates-Généraux.* . . . Also appears as *Edict dv Roy svr la Pacification des trovbles de ce Royaume,* May 1576, in French Political Pamphlets in the Newberry Library (Lindsay and Neu, no. 881).

[204]*Edict de Pacification faict par le Roy pour mettre fin aux Troubles de son Royaume, & faire desormais viure tous ses subiects en bonne paix, vnion & concorde, soubs son obeissance,* Paris 1578, 19–20, reissued 1595. In the French Political Pamphlets in the Newberry Library (Lindsay and Neu, no. 939 and the reissue, no. 1990).

[205]*Arrest de la covrt des grandz Iours seant en la Ville de Poictiers,* Poitiers 1579, in the French Political Pamphlets in the Newberry Library (Lindsay and Neu, no. 980).

[206]*Edict du Roy sur la Pacification des troubles, contenant confirmation, ampliation, & declaration, tant des precedents Edicts sur ledit faict, mesmes en l'an 1577, que des Articles arrestez en la Conference de Nerac,* 26 January 1581, Paris, in French Political Pamphlets in the Newberry Library (Lindsay and Neu, no. 1011).

[207]*De L'Acord et Remonstrance qve le Roy a faict à tous ses subjectz, qui sont sous son obeissance,* Paris, no date, probably 1583, in French Political Pamphlets in the Newberry Library (Lindsay and Neu, no. 1043).

TOWARDS *UNE FOI, UN ROI, UNE LOI?*

As early as 1583 (even before the death of Henry III's brother and heir presumptive, Francis, Duke of Anjou and Alençon), Henry of Guise was accused of claiming a right to the throne of France. This charge appeared in the work of Philippe Duplessis-Mornay, *Discovrs svr le Droit Pretendu par ceux de Guise sur la Couronne de France.*[208] The Catholic League of 1576 had dissolved into indifference because its members and supporters had no immediately pressing issue around which they could sustain an active union. However, Anjou died in 1584 and the Protestant Henry of Navarre became heir presumptive under traditional succession rules. Now the end of the Valois line and the succession of the Bourbon "heretic" seemed imminent. A new, stronger Catholic League formed around this issue. Its members felt that it would be intolerable for a heretic to succeed to the throne of Catholic France. This fear was intensified by Henry III's apparent support of the Protestant faction: "Nevertheless since the death of Monsieur, brother of the King, the demands of those who by public profession have shown themselves persecutors of the Catholic Church, have been so supported and favored. . . ."[209]

The League's supporters interpreted the royal coronation oath's clause requiring the king to protect the faith as an exclusion of all heretics (defined by them as non-Catholics) from the royal succession. Since a heretic could not be a king to Catholic France, the Catholic faction put forth a claim on behalf of Charles, the Cardinal of Bourbon and uncle of Henry of Navarre, as right-

---

[208]*Discovrs svr le Droit Pretendu par ceux de Guise sur la Couronne de France*, 1583, in French Political Pamphlets in the Newberry Library (Lindsay and Neu, no. 1054). For an excellent biography of the king's brother Francis, Duke of Anjou and a discussion of the times, see Mack Holt, *The Duke of Anjou and the Politique Struggle during the Wars of Religion* (New York: Cambridge University Press, 1986).

[209]*Declaration. Des causes qui ont mû Monseigneur le Cardinal de Bourbon & les Pairs, Princes, Prelatz, Seigneurs, Villes & Communautez de ce Royaume de veulent subuertir la religion & l'Estat*, 1585, in Simon Goulart, *Mémoires de la Ligue, contenant les évenemens les plus remarquables depuis 1576, jusqu'à la paix accordée entre le roi de France et le roi d'Espagne en 1598*, new edition by Goujet (Amsterdam: Arkstée and Merkus, 1758), tome 1, 57: "Toutefois depuis la mort de Monseigneur Frere du Roi, les prétentions de ceux qui par profession, publique se sont toujours, montres persecuteurs de l'Eglise Catholique, ont été tellement favorisées & appuyées. . . ." Also in French Political Pamphlets in the Newberry Library (Lindsay and Neu, no. 1089).

ful heir to the throne and protector of the Catholic faith in France.[210] The Leaguer Catholics, though prepared to fight for their cause, declared in the Second Declaration of Péronne that they were not taking arms against the king, but were actually defending him:

Affirming that it is not against the King our sovereign Lord that we take arms, but for the protection and defense of his person, of his life and of his estate, for which we swear and pledge all, to risk our goods and our lives, until the last drop of our blood, with fidelity equal to that which we have had in the past: and to put aside our arms as soon as it will have pleased his Majesty to make an end to the danger that threatens the destruction of the service of God and of so many men of property.[211]

The king, faced with disruption by private warfare and still responsible for maintaining public order as his medieval predecessors had been, responded to attempts to raise such private armies with an edict ordering them to lay down their arms and disband immediately, under penalty of punishment to the fullest extent of his ordinance:

We have declared and we declare by these present, that if there are any who . . . without our commission dispatched under our great seal, have made levies of men of war, either of foot soldiers or of horse, they are to desist from it immediately, to discharge them and send them back. . . .[212]

The Catholic refusal to accept Henry of Navarre as heir presumptive to the French throne extended beyond his being a heretic to the fear that Catholicism would be eliminated under him in the same way that the radical Catholics wished to see Protestantism eradicated under Henry III.[213] In 1585 Pope Sixtus V de-

---

[210]Ibid.

[211]Ibid., 61: "Protestant que ce n'est contre le Roi notre souverain Seigneur que prenons les armes, ains pour la tuition & défense de sa personne, de sa vie & de son Etat, pour lequel nous jurons & promettons tous exposer nos biens & nos vies, jusqu'à la derniere guotte de notre sang, avec pareille fidelité qu'avons fait par le passé: & de poser les armes aussitôt, qu'il aura plu à sa Majesté faire cesser le péril qui menace la ruine du service de Dieu & de tant de gens de bien. . . ."

[212]Edit du roi, sur la Défense des armes, qu'il fait contre se sont ligués en son Royaume, 28 March 1585, in Mémoires de la Ligue, tome 1, 54–56. The quotation is from 55: "Nous avons declaré & declarons par ces présentes, que s'il y a aucuns qui . . . sans nos commissions expédiées sous notre grand scel, aient fait des levées de gens de guerre, soit à pied ou à cheval, ils aient à s'en désister promptement, les licencier & renvoyer. . . ."

[213]Victor de Chalambert, Histoire de la Ligue sous les règnes de Henri III et Henri IV, ou quinze années de l'histoire de France (Paris, 1898; rp. Geneva: Slatkine-Megariotis, 1974), 2–4.

clared both Henry of Navarre and Condé heretics. Since some medieval Church writers had argued that heretics could not hold property and Christian subjects did not have to obey heretic kings, this declaration was, in effect, the confiscation of Henry of Navarre's future inheritance, the kingdom of France. Henry III proceeded to declare Catholicism the only religion of France in a royal edict of July 1585[214] and gave the Huguenots the choice of converting within six months or leaving France. The penalties for doing neither consisted of imprisonment and confiscation of goods. Reaffirmed in October of the same year, the edict stated that no longer would there be:

any exercise of the new so-called reformed religion, but only that of our Catholic, Apostolic, and Roman religion. That we prevent and forbid [the Reformed religion] very expressly to all our subjects of whatever property and condition that they be, under pain of confiscation of body and of goods, not withstanding the permission which was given to do this by our preceding edicts of pacification, which we have revoked and are revoking by these present ones. . . . [215]

The revocation of the previous acts of toleration suggests the influence and pressure under which the Papacy and the French Catholics had placed Henry III.

The belief in the necessity of the one religion of Roman Catholicism caused French writers to be influenced by religious concepts and to view the break in the unity of religion as dangerous not only to religious values, but to the State itself. The two fundamental principles of the Catholic League were based on this belief. For the Leaguers, the Salic law regulated the succession to the Crown and assured the continuity of kings and kingdom; the Catholicity of the French king and nation assured the continuity of the king as the Lord's anointed, as the "Most Christian King" and as the "Eldest Son of the Church." The League of 1576 was directed mainly at Henry III's tolerance and even favoritism for

---

[214]Isambert, vol. 14, part II, p. 595, no. 290, July 1585, *Edit qui révoque ceux de pacification, et qui enjoint à tous les sujets du roi de professer la religion catholique.* Also in *Mémoires de la Ligue,* vol. 1, 178–182.

[215]Ibid., in *Mémoires de la Ligue,* tome 1, 179: ". . . il ne se fera dorénavant aucun exercice de la nouvelle Religion prétendue réformée, mais seulement celui de notre Religion Catholique, Apostolique & Romaine. Ce que nous inhibons & défendons très expressément à tous nos Sujets de quelque qualité & condition qu'ils soient, sur peine de confiscation de corps & de beins, nonobstant la permission qui étoit donnée de ce faire par nos Edits de pacification precedens, laquelle nous avons révoquée & révoquons par ces présentes. . . ."

the Huguenot and politique[216] elements in the kingdom, but the real problem for French Catholics did not arise until the death in 1584 of Henry III's younger brother, heir presumptive to the throne. It was not until 1584 and 1585 that they saw Henry of Bourbon, Huguenot king of Navarre, as a threat to the essential nature of France and her people. The argument against Henry of Navarre as heir was simple: a heretic, particularly a relapsed heretic such as Henry, could never fulfill his coronation oath and therefore could never be a lawful king of France. They were willing to justify almost any action if its purpose was to resist a heretic king or the succession of a heretic to the throne.

The religious argument was important on all sides. Even though the Huguenots' and politiques' support of Henry of Navarre was based firmly on juristic and dynastic grounds of succession, they felt it necessary to address the religious question in such a way that moderate Catholics at least would give Navarre their support. Quentin Skinner has shown that much of Huguenot ideology was influenced by late medieval "Catholic" political thought and would be quite familiar and even acceptable to the moderates and the uncommitted.[217] Another approach was to deny that Huguenots were heretics. One 1585 pamphlet defined heresy pragmatically as a major error which went to the very foundation of faith. The pamphlet went on to argue that the King of Navarre was a Christian who believed in the same basic tenets of Christianity as French Catholics did: finding salvation in Jesus Christ, believing His word was infallible truth, revering the symbols of the Church, accepting the universal councils of the Church, and condemning the heresies denounced by the councils.[218] Even at this date, there was still a feeling that Chris-

---

[216]The politiques in sixteenth-century France were not an organized political party in any sense. The movement was composed of Huguenots and many moderate Catholics who shared a belief in freedom of conscience in religion. This was based on pragmatism rather than principle. The politiques' main concern was with the preservation of the French state and they were willing to accept religious toleration as preferable to continued civil warfare. For the use of the word 'politique' in the sixteenth century, see Holt, *The Duke of Anjou*, 2, note 4. For a full description of the relationship of the politiques to other groups, see Jouanna, ch. 6, especially 166–174 and the diagram on 167.

The role of the politiques was seen in various ways by contemporaries: " 'Politiques' . . . are those who give more to men than to God." (Jacques Charpentier, 1569) was one view; another was: " 'Politiques' are those who do not want to dip their hands in the blood of Christians." (Pierre du Belloy, 1587). Both quoted in Donald R. Kelley, *François Hotman: A Revolutionary's Ordeal* (Princeton: Princeton University Press, 1973), 327.

[217]Skinner, "Origins of the Calvinist Theory," 325.

[218]*Responce avx Declarations & protestations de Messieurs de Guise, faictes sous le nom de Monseigneur le Cardinal de Bourbon, pour justifier leur iniuste prise des armes*, 1585, 32–33, in French Political Pamphlets in the Newberry Library (Lindsay and Neu, no. 1116).

tianity could once again be made whole. This same pamphlet suggested the calling of a universal council and insisted that no schism existed since a schism assumed a resolve to separate. If a council were held, reunion would follow.[219] Furthermore, heresy presupposes an intention at novelty, an opinion against reason which has been taught and demonstrated. The King of Navarre did not exhibit these characteristics.[220]

The moderate tone of this pamphlet and of Belloy's *Apologie catholique* more accurately represented the moderate position of many of the pamphleteers who supported the cause of religious toleration. The motivation for religious toleration generally did not come from ideological conviction, but from political pragmatism. Supporters of toleration followed the Church's traditional view that the only justifiable basis for permitting heresy was necessity.[221] Politiques were not just hopeful Huguenots, but included many moderate Catholics and some who drifted back and forth from Catholicism to Protestantism as did Henry of Navarre.[222]

Catholics continued to complain about the violence in the realm and blamed the king for not stopping it. A 1586 plea to the king by a "gentleman of the Church" charged that the king's subjects had been pillaged and killed, without any appearance of justice and the author went on to tell the king once again of the miseries of his subjects:

Haven't they entered, sacked, murdered, and killed your poor subjects without procedure nor form of justice, to avenge their private injuries under the shadow of Religion, as though it is injury done to them when one adheres to yours and to your obedience: . . . You turn away your ears and your eyes from the just quarrel and lamentation of a great

---

[219]Ibid., 33.

[220]Ibid., 34. Belloy had included similar arguments in his *Apologie catholique.*

[221]E.M. Beame, "The Limits of Toleration in Sixteenth-Century France," *Studies in the Renaissance* 13 (1966): 251.

[222]Etienne Pasquier, for example, remained a Catholic throughout his life and during the Wars of Religion he remained loyal to the monarchy [Vittorio de Caprariis, *Propaganda e pensiero politico in Francia durante le guerre di religione*, vol. I, 1559–1572 (Naples: Edizioni scientifiche italiane, 1959), 290–291.] The dispute over whether he was in favor of religious toleration or opposed to it seems to depend largely on the question of the authorship of the anonymous pamphlet *Exhortation aux Princes*. His biographer and editor Dorothy Thickett credits him with authorship and claims that he was a proponent of religious tolerance. Most other contributors to the debate do not consider this his work, and thus place him in the camp of those who wished France to remain a nation of 'une foi, un roi, une loi' and believed this would happen naturally, given peace. Thus the unwillingness to extirpate Protestantism violently does not necessarily mark an acceptance of religious plurality. [For a short summary and bibliography on the question of Pasquier's religious tolerance or intolerance, see Myriam Yardeni, *La conscience nationale en France pendant les guerres de religion (1559–1598)* (Louvain: Editions Nauwelaerts, 1971), 84–85, note 22.]

troop of widows and orphans: and not only that, but you hold the guilty ones beside Your Majesty as in safeguard, against God, against the holy laws and justice, which cries vengeance to him. And this great God from whom you hold all that which you have, will He maintain your rule in this great injustice?[223]

This piece, addressed to Henry III, reminds him that he is still under God's divine law, however he may act above human law. Instead of maintaining public order, he is letting his people suffer and protecting their persecutors. He owes it to his loyal followers, specifically he owes it to the followers of the Catholic faith, not to protect their enemies which are, the author feels, the king's enemies as well. God will not long tolerate injustice, even, or especially, from a king.

While Catholics charged the Protestants with atrocities and numerous crimes,[224] the Huguenots defended their own use of armed force which they still claimed was only to "guarantee and defend the King, . . . and all the good Frenchmen from the oppression of enemies conspiring against this crown. . ." and to fight a defensive war against the men of war who caused misery and calamities to the people.[225]

Henry III fully recognized the threat of the League and of the Guise family at the meeting of the Estates at Blois in 1588, although he could not successfully resist their influence at the time. He eventually responded to Guise and his implicit threat to

---

[223]*Au Roi, mon souverain seigneur. Sur les miseres du temps present & de la conspiration des Ennemis de sa Majesté. Par un Gentilhomme de l'Eglise,* 1586, in *Mémoires de la Ligue,* tome 2, 101: "N'ont-ils pas, d'entrée, saccagé, meurtri & tué vos pauvres sujets sans forme ni figure de justice, pour venger leurs injures privées sous ombre de la Religion, si c'est injure faite à eux quand on se tient des votres & de votre obeissance. . . . Vous detournez vos oreilles & vos yeux de la querelle & plainte tant juste d'une grande troupe de veuves & d'orphelins: & non seulement cela, mais tenez les coupables auprès de votre Majesté comme en sauvegarde, contre Dieu, contre les saintes Loix, & la justice, qui lui crient vengeance. Et ce grand Dieu de qui vous tenez tout ce que vous avez, maintiendra-t-il votre domination en si grande injustice?" Further complaints about the general discord in the realm appear in *Exhortation et Remonstrance, faite d'vn commvn accord par les françois Catholiques & Pacifiques, pour la paix,* 1586, in French Political Pamphlets in the Newberry Library (Lindsay and Neu, no. 1150).

[224]*Discovrs d'vn vertvevx Catholiqve qvi est vne iuste & vraye deffense de la Maiesté tres-Chrestienne & ample response contre ses capitaux ennemis; des heretiques du iourd'huy, leurs grandes & atroces iniures, calomnies, maldisances, trahisons, machinations, & coniurations tresiniques & desseins fort à craindre & à redouter,* 1587, in French Political Pamphlets in the Newberry Library (Lindsay and Neu, no. 1165).

[225]*Protestation et Declaration dv Roy de Nauarre, sur la venue de son armee en France,* 1587, in French Political Pamphlets in the Newberry Library (Lindsay and Neu, no. 1185): ". . . l'occasion [sic] de le prinse de noz armes, n'auoir esté que pour guarentir & deffendre le Roy . . . & tous les bons Frauçois [sic] de l'oppression des ennemis coniurez de ceste Couronne. . ." and ". . . mais vne guerre deffensive, nous contenans en noz places, sans nous mettre aucunement aux champs, tant pour soulager le pauure peuple des miseres & calamitez que les gens de guerre, quelque disciplinez qu'ils soient, luy causent."

the royal sovereignty by having him assassinated on 23 December 1588; this murder was followed by that of Guise's brother, the Cardinal of Guise, on the next day. The king simultaneously imprisoned Charles, the Cardinal of Bourbon, who was the League's choice as royal heir; the Duke's young son; and numerous other handy and important Leaguers. Unfortunately for the king, the third Guise brother, the Duke of Mayenne, escaped the net and became the rallying point for the next phase of the Catholic opposition.

The assassinations (or executions) of the Duke of Guise and the Cardinal of Guise on the orders of Henry III made the latter a tyrant in the eyes of many. Many people who had previously supported Henry III could no longer do so in good conscience. He tried to defend his actions by repeating the argument that the king is above the law, deriving from this legal formula a right to execute rebels arbitrarily. This use of the medieval adaptation of the Roman law, which made the king "emperor in his own kingdom" did nothing to gain him support. Although Roman law could be used in this way to strengthen the claims of the monarchy, other Roman law principles could be used with the opposite effect.

The idea of popular sovereignty had become increasingly common with the medieval revival of Roman law. Writers commenting on the Roman civil law interpreted the *Lex regia* passages of Justinian's *Digest* as meaning that the emperor's or king's authority originally came from the people. This meant that in addition to being a tyrant, a king could also be a traitor. On 8 January 1589 the theological faculty of the Sorbonne, under pressure from the Catholic preachers of the radical Paris Sixteen, formally declared Henry III himself guilty of *lèse-majesté* and declared him deposed as king of France.[226] This act was designed to free the people from their allegiance to him and to authorize their taking up arms against him; it echoed the arguments put forth in the earlier radical Huguenot treatise, the *Vindiciae contra tyrannos*. Further justification came from Henry III's returning to the support of Navarre as his heir to the French throne.

Calls for a Catholic rebellion gained more support in May 1589 when news of the Papal Bull of excommunication pronounced

---

[226]Under this pressure, the Sorbonne deposed Henry III in January 1589, even before the pope acted. The Sorbonne's statement declared that "Frenchmen can take up arms, raise money and band together for the Catholic, apostolic and Roman religion against a king who has violated the public faith in the assembly of the estates." Quoted from J.H.M. Salmon, "The Paris Sixteen, 1584–94: The Social Analysis of a Revolutionary Movement," *Journal of Modern History* 44 (December 1972): 555–556.

against Henry III reached France. This Bull was translated into French and widely circulated.[227] Opponents of Henry III accepted his excommunication as a virtual deposition and began to identify him as "Henry of Valois" rather than as "Henry III, King of France." He was a heretic now and his opponents openly accused his supporters, and those of the Bourbon heir Henry of Navarre, who had been excommunicated in 1585, of being guilty of two types of *lèse-majesté:* divine and human.[228] The Bull caused a double response, however. Although strong Catholic League members and their supporters could use it as further justification for their cause, more moderate Gallican Catholics saw the Bull as an attempt by the Pope to meddle in French affairs.

After Henry III's assassinations of the duke and the Cardinal of Guise in 1588 and his resulting excommunication, Catholic writers such as Jean Boucher drew upon the earlier Huguenot arguments of elective kingship, especially the idea of a covenant as developed in the *Vindiciae contra tyrannos*. This latter work had argued that the people would obey the king if he were a proper ruler. In some cases repeating the Protestant arguments almost verbatim,[229] the Catholic writers used them to support their own theories of rights to rebel and the elective nature of kingship. According to their arguments, if one accepted the necessity of the coronation ceremony in the making of a king, it became virtually impossible for a non-Catholic to become king of France.[230] In addition to his having to convince representatives of the Catholic nation to "elect" him, he would also have to swear to root out heresy. If he failed in the first, he would not become king; if he failed in the second, he would break the contract of the "election" and the people would have the right to overthrow him. The Catholic writers, as the Huguenot, medieval Christian, and Ro-

---

[227]*Bulle de nostre S. Pere le Pape Sixte V, contre Henry de Valois, & ses complices*, 1589, in French Political Pamphlets in the Newberry Library (Lindsay and Neu, no. 1421).

[228]For example, *Arrest de la Cour de Parlement de Paris contre ceux qui tiennent le party de Henry de Bourbon, declaré heretique par nostre S. Pere le Pape, & qui luy prestent ayde, secours & faueur*, Paris 1589, in French Political Pamphlets in the Newberry Library (Lindsay and Neu, no. 1492). It is important to realize that the Parlement of Paris had been split into two factions in 1588 when the king had been forced to flee from Paris. A "rump" parlement continued to sit in Paris as the Parlement of Paris and was generally controlled by the Catholic radicals in the Paris Sixteen. Many other members eventually escaped the city and joined the king, who established a rival Parlement at Tours in 1589. The Parlement sitting at Tours declared the papal bull against Henry III contrary to the liberties of the Gallican Church. See J.H. Shennan, *The Parlement of Paris* (Ithaca: Cornell University Press, 1968), 227–228.

[229]Jackson, 162.

[230]Jean Boucher, *De iusta Henri Tertii: Abdicatione e francorum regno*, 2nd ed. (Paris: N. Niuellium, 1589) is the best-known expression of these arguments, although the work was not published until after Henry III's assassination in August 1589.

man law writers before them, based their arguments on the ideas
of contract in private law. A key feature of any contract is that it
binds both parties and if one party breaks it, the other is no
longer bound. If the king broke his part of the contract he made
at his coronation or "election," his people were freed from their
contract with him.

Those who supported Henry of Navarre as heir to the French
throne responded to the excommunication and to Boucher's arguments in one of two ways. They either denied the pope power
to excommunicate in France, as François Hotman had done,[231] or
they denied that Calvinism was in any way heretical to begin
with, as Pierre de Belloy had done in his *Apologie catholique*. Belloy argued that there would be no problem with the coronation of
Henry of Navarre because he was not a heretic. Henry was a
Christian and did not profess beliefs condemned by any legitimate ecumenical council of the Church.[232] Belloy could use this
argument because the French, or Gallican, Catholic Church had
never accepted the decrees of the Council of Trent, which laid the
foundation for charges that Protestantism was heresy.

In a 1589 pamphlet critical of Henry III, the author, who
claimed to be speaking for Catholics, argued that the people were
oppressed, there was contempt for the sovereign courts, justice
was being sold, benefices were dispensed unjustly, the nobility
was badly recognized, and the gendarmerie recompensed poorly
or not at all. Further, there was an excessive number of royal officers to support a tyranny better, an unbelievable number of
edicts, "tending to no other end than to draw in the money;
which ought to incite, indeed to compel, all men of property, of
whatever quality or condition that they may be, to arm themselves to restore the state to better order."[233] Clearly, the king was
neither maintaining public order nor protecting his subjects and
their property as he had sworn to do at his coronation. He was

---

[231]François Hotman, *P. Sixti V. Fvlmen Brvtum. In Henricvm sereniss, Regem Nauarrae, &
illustriss Henricvm Borbonium, Principem olim Conaeum, euibratum*, (n.p. 1586).

[232]Belloy, *Apologie catholiqve*, fol. 75v.

[233]*Causes qui ont contraint les Catholiques à prendre les armes*, in *Mémoires de la Ligue*, 1589,
tome 3, 527: "Bref, Messieurs, l'oppression du pauvre Peuple, qui gemit toujours sous ce
joug insupportable, le mépris des Cours Souveraines, la Justice vendue, les Bénéfices in-
justement despensés, la Noblesse mal reconnue, la Gendarmerie peu ou point recom-
pensée, encore qu'on leve tant de deniers sous ce prétexte, le désordre & confusion des
Etats, tant Séculiers qu'Ecclésiastiques, le nombre excessif des Officiers pour mieux
appuïer une tyrannie, la multitude incroïable des Edits, ne tendant tous à autre fin qu'à
tirer de l'argent, doivent exciter voire contraindre tous les hommes de bien, de quelque
qualité ou condition qu'ils soient, s'armer pour remettre l'Etat en meilleur ordre." Also in
French Political Pamphlets in the Newberry Library (Lindsay and Neu, no. 1427).

not fulfilling his part of the contract. If the milder forms of *requêtes* and remonstrances failed to bring about change, it would be necessary to take the drastic measure of calling the Estates, "the last ordinary remedy, as much for the king as for the people."[234] These complaints are clearly secular in nature and were presumably included to appeal to a larger audience of moderate Catholics, the same audience the Huguenot pamphleteers were trying to reach.

Referring to the coronation oath, the same pamphleteer went on to say, "The people made the kings and submitted itself voluntarily to their power; when they [the kings] abuse it [power], it [the people] can pull them down as easily as it created them."[235] This step, he said, should be taken by the people meeting in the Estates, not by individuals, and only after less severe methods have failed to bring about change. This radical step had been suggested earlier by Calvinist resistance theorists, especially the anonymous author of the *Discours politiques* who had devised a procedure which allowed for the deposition and trial of the king, as well as for his assassination if he refused to submit to judgment. It was another revival of the popular sovereignty theories.

The combination of the Sorbonne's 1589 deposition of Henry III and their declaration that he was guilty of *lèse majesté*, as well as the Papal Bull of excommunication made it possible for some to oppose the king openly without feeling that they were committing *lèse majesté* themselves.[236] Many people still felt that greater authority was necessary, however, before they could legally resort to open rebellion. They felt that the requirement of "proper authority" necessary for a just war had not yet been met. A meeting of the Estates was "the last ordinary remedy, as much for the kings as for the people," said the author of *Causes qui ont contraint les Catholiques à prendre les armes*, and he did not "leave to the people the power to punish the kings when they abuse their dignity, but to the assembly of the most virtuous personnages of the kingdom, to the deputies of the three Estates of each province, after

---

[234]Ibid., 527: "Quand on a essaié les plus douces voies, comme requêtes & remontrances, on s'en est moqué; enfin on l'a contraint d'assembler les Etats, qui est, le dernier remede des ordinaires, tant pour les Rois que pour le Peuple."

[235]Ibid., 528: "Le Peuple a fait les Rois, il s'est volontairement soumis à leur puissance; quand ils en abuseront, il peut aussi aisement les défaire comme il les a crées."

[236]Ibid., 523: "Nous devons, dis-je, pardoner les injures particulières, quand elles n'importent qu'à nous-mêmes; mais quand il y va de l'honneur de Dieu & du Public, il faut s'armer pour si juste querelle. . . ."

having tried the more gentle remedies."[237] This move to correct the erring king was not only a right but a duty. Once a king had failed to carry out his duties to protect his kingdom and had given aid and comfort to heretics, he forfeited his claim to the kingdom.

In the Catholic justification for the new wars, there was a repetition of the medieval requirements for just war. First, war should be undertaken only by necessity because, "one does not look for peace, he [St. Augustine] said, to practice war, but one makes war to obtain peace."[238] The Catholic war referred to was a just one because it was preferable to peace with the heretics. But according to the theory developed in the Middle Ages, a just war must be conducted by a legitimate authority. Ordinarily this would be the secular ruler or king, but what if he would not fight? The author of the pamphlet dealt with this problem too:

But if the Prince is absent when it is a question of the defense of peace and of the people, or if being present, he does not wish or is not able to defend the side of God. . . . If the Prince, then, instead of doing his duty would be so forgetful, as to show himself more Tyrant than King, more heretic than Catholic, more enemy of the true religion than propagator and defender . . . the subject is not held to await the return or the convenience of his Prince, but can, even must, do his duty to defend himself and his country against the incursion of the enemy.[239]

According to this view, the need to defend oneself or one's country overcomes the need for a legitimate authority to conduct a

---

[237]Ibid., 528–529: "Je ne laisse donc pas la puissance de châtier les Rois quand ils abusent de leur dignité au populace indiscret; mais à l'assemblée des plus vertueux personnages de tout le Roïaume, au Deputés des trois Etats de chaque Province, après avoir essaïé les plus doux remedes."

[238]*Ivstification de la gverre entreprise, commencee et povrsvivie sovz la conduicte de tresvaleureux & debonnaire Prince Monseigneur le Duc de Mayenne*, Paris 1589, 6, in French Political Pamphlets in the Newberry Library (Lindsay and Neu, no. 1546): ". . . lon ne cherche pas la paix, dit il [St. Augustine], pour exercer la guerre, mais on fait la guerre pour obtenir paix. Mais que ceste guerre Catholique, dont nous parlons, soit entreprise sans aucune necessité, ne le nie tout à plat, & afferme, que s'il s'est oncques trouue iuste occasion de faire guerre, elle se trouue en ceste guerre entreprise par les Catholiques. Car tant s'en faut que la paix euë auec les heretiques en vertu de l'Edict de Pacification se doiue appeller paix, que nous deuons preferer toute forte de guerre a telle paix." It should be noted here that St. Augustine did not consider a desire for peace to be a just cause for war, since all wars were fought for peace and each side defined peace in its own terms.

[239]Ibid., 16–19: "Mais si le Prince est absent lors qu'il est question de la defense du païs & du peuple, ou si estant present, il ne veut, ou ne peut defendre la querelle de Dieu . . . Si le Prince donc, au lieu de faire son deuoir se seroit tant oublié, que de se monstrer plustost Tyran que Roy, heretique que Catholique, ennemy de la vraye religion, que propugnateur & defendeur . . . le subiet n'est pas tenu d'attendre le retour ou commodité de son Prince, ains peut, voire doit faire son deuoir de se defendre & sa patrie contre l'incursion de l'ennemy."

war, and this agrees with the common legal view of self-defense, that immediate danger may be repulsed without appeal to authority. It is interesting to see that the appeal is to self-defense instead of to the pope to call a crusade against the French heretics. This must be understood not only in the context of secular law, but also in the context of Gallican Catholicism, which resented foreign interference in France. Although radical League Catholics were willing to accept Italian and Spanish aid, moderate Catholics would be more susceptible to the secular argument of self-defense. From another perspective, this could be seen as a case of popular sovereignty, where ultimately authority would lie with the people, at least when the king failed to act.

On the other hand, some believed that royal power came from God and that the reigning king ought to be held "sacrosanct, inviolate and holy, and we ought to give him all honor and obedience."[240] To take arms against the king was to take arms against God: "the status of the Kings, Sire, is sacred, their power bound with that of God, those who carry arms against them, carry arms against God, and take not the road of salvation, but of damnation. . . ."[241]

The Catholic League, and most of those who felt that Henry of Navarre could not be king of France because he was a heretic, continued to support Charles, Cardinal of Bourbon as the legitimate heir. After the assassination of Henry III in 1589, they supported the cardinal as the new King Charles X. His right as heir had been repeatedly mentioned ever since the death of the Duke of Anjou in 1584 and had been recognized by Henry III in 1588, before the king imprisoned him.[242] With the assassination of Henry III, Henry of Navarre also claimed his right to succession and, taking the title Henry IV against the opposition of the Catholic party, he tried to rule France as its king. His Protestantism

---

[240]*Remonstrance avx François svr levr sedition, rebellion et felonnie, contre la Majesté du Roy,* 1589, 6, in French Political Pamphlets in the Newberry Library (not listed in Lindsay and Neu):" . . . & à nostre Roy regnant, doiuent estre tenus par nous sacro-saints, inuiolables & sacrez, & leur deuons rendre tout honneur & obeissance."

[241]*Remonstrance av Roy Henry III, du nom, Roy de France & de Pologne, & aux Estats generaux de France à Bloys. Faict par le sieur de Sindré, l'vn des deputez de la Noblesse de Bourbonnois.,* Lyon 1589, 5–6, in French Political Pamphlets in the Newberry Library (Lindsay and Neu, no. 1649): ". . . l'estat des Roys, Sire, est sacré, leur puissance liee auec celle de Dieu, ceux qui portent les armes contre luy, portent les armes contre Dieu, & ne prennent la voye de salut, mais de damnation. . . ."

[242]*De la Svccession dv droict et prerogative de premier Prince du sang de France, deferée par la loy du Royaume, à Monseigneur Charles Cardinal de Bourbon, par le mort de Monseigneur François de Valois Duc d'Anjou,* in French from the Latin treatise of Matthew Zampini, *Pro svccessione praerogativae primi principis, per legem Regni, Cardinali Borbonio delatae,* Paris 1589, both in French Political Pamphlets in the Newberry Library (Lindsay and Neu, nos. 1668 and 1669).

remained a burning issue, and for some devout Catholics he could never be a legitimate king since he was not only a heretic, but a relapsed heretic. He began to issue royal edicts reestablishing the Edicts of Pacification which Henry III had withdrawn under pressure from the League[243] and to revoke edicts which the League had issued to usurp royal power.[244]

In an attempt to obtain peace and support for his rule, Henry IV tried to reassure the Catholics in the kingdom that their religion was respected and protected: "We will not change, nor innovate, nor allow any change or innovation to the practice and exercise of the Catholic, Apostolic, and Roman Religion, which we wish to preserve and maintain, as well as those who profess it, in all their authority, franchises, and liberties. . . ."[245] This declaration was necessary because many of those still in rebellion against Henry IV opposed him on the grounds that a non-Catholic king would persecute them. Henry IV was demonstrating, even before he took the coronation oath, that he intended to protect the faith of the Catholics in his kingdom. Those who opposed him for political reasons, however, still used the religious issue to encourage rebellion against him, as a 1591 pamphlet pointed out: "[The rebels] seeing that our King has not yet made himself a Catholic, take pleasure in these remonstrances, as justification for their rebellion."[246] The Duke of Mayenne (the surviving Guise brother), led the Catholic opposition forces and continued to fuel the flames of rebellion on religious grounds, with reminders that the fundamental law of the kingdom required that "the prince who claims right to the Crown by proximity of blood must be Catholic as an essential and necessary

---

[243]*Edict dv Roy, Contenant restablissement des Edicts de Pacification faicts par le deffunct Roy Henry, troisiesme sur les troubles de ce Royaume*, published by the Cour de Parlement sitting at Challons, 24 July 1591, in French Political Pamphlets in the Newberry Library (Lindsay and Neu, no. 1750).

[244]*Edict dv Roy svr la revocation des edicts de·la Ligue, faits és années mil cinq cens quatre vingts cinq, & quatre vingts huict*, Tours 1591, in French Political Pamphlets in the Newberry Library (Lindsay and Neu, no. 1751).

[245]*Declaration dv Roy confirmative d'avtre Declaration par luy faicte à son aduenement a la Couronne, de vouloir maintenir & conseruer la Religion Catholique, Apostolique & Romaine*, Tours 1591, 7, in French Political Pamphlets in the Newberry Library (Lindsay and Neu, no. 1749): "Ayant ce pendant iuré & promis que nous ne changérions ou innouerions ny ne souffririons estre rien change ou innoué, au faict & exercice de la Religion Catholique, Apostolique & Romaine, laquelle nous voulions conseruer & maintenir, & ceux qui font profession d'icelle, en toutes leurs authoritez, franchises & libertez. . . ."

[246]*Responce à la svpplication, contre celvy lequel faisant semblant de donner aduis au Roy de se faire Catholic veult exciter ses bons subiects à rebellion*, 1591, 4–5, in French Political Pamphlets in the Newberry Library (Lindsay and Neu, no. 1762): ". . . la pluspart sont rebelles . . . voyans que nostre Roy ne s'est fait encores Catholic, prennent plaisir à ces remonstrance, comme piece iustificatiue de leur rebellion. . . ."

quality to be King of a Kingdom. . . ."[247] Protecting Catholicism was not enough for him; the king must also be Catholic himself.

In May 1590 the Catholic League's "king," Charles X (the aged Cardinal of Bourbon), died in captivity. An old man when he was declared king, he had never ruled outside of prison, and had instead been used by Mayenne to legitimate his own claim as lieutenant-general of France. For the League, the death of "king" Charles opened up the entire succession question once again, since his legal heir would ordinarily have been his closest male relative, his nephew Henry of Navarre, whom the League had already rejected. There was no legal basis for Mayenne's next step. To settle the succession problem, Mayenne called an Estates General to elect a new king. Traditionally, the Estates General was a consultative body which only the king could call into session. Now there was no king.

For Mayenne to call the Estates was therefore a radical step not only because he was playing the role of the king, but because he was changing the function of the Estates from consulting with the king to electing the king. As a body supposedly representing the kingdom, the Estates could be seen as representing the people, the election as the practice of popular sovereignty. The Estates never accomplished their radical goal, however. The succession question became so complicated and involved so much foreign intrigue that the issue precipitated the demise of the organized Catholic opposition.

The League's Estates of 1593 hardly represented all of France; it represented only certain areas and certain interest groups. The Duke of Feria presented the claims of Philip II of Spain whose objectives centered around the French abrogating the Salic law to allow the succession of Philip's daughter, the Infanta Isabelle-Claire-Eugénie, granddaughter of Henry II of France and niece of Henry III.[248] Many delegates to the Estates saw this as an attempt at foreign usurpation and the issue caused some of the moderate Catholics to look more favorably on the possible acceptance of Henry IV, if he would convert to Catholicism. A contributing factor to the defeat of the Spanish intentions came with the declaration of the Parlement of Paris, stated in unequivocal terms, that

---

[247]*Declaration faite par Monseigneur le Duc de Mayenne, Lieutenant-Général de l'Etat & Couronne de France, pour la réunion de tous les Catholiques de ce Roiaume*, 1592, 4–5, in *Mémoires de la Ligue*, tome 5, 270: ". . . & la Loi fondamentale du Roiaume, qui requiert au Prince qui prétend droit à la Couronne, avec la proximité du sang, qu'il soit Catholic, comme qualité essentielle & necessaire pour être Roi d'un Roiaume. . . ."

[248]Albert Mousset, "Les droits de l'infante Isabelle-Claire-Eugénie à la couronne de France," *Bulletin hispanique* 16 (1914): 46–79.

under no circumstances could the Salic law be set aside.[249] The Catholic League itself no longer had the strength it once had had. Since 1589 it had declined as a formidable political and military force, in part because of the defection of numerous nobles.

The meeting of the Estates and the debates over the succession brought out into the open the true nature of Spain's intentions in France. It became difficult even for the most ardent Catholics to see the Spanish king Philip's goals as merely oriented for universal Catholicism; he clearly had dynastic dreams of his own in France. Supporting a foreign Catholic for king now appeared to be *lèse-majesté* against the kingdom of France. Increasingly, support of the League and its Estates appeared to be treason. A foreign Catholic as king of France was as bad, or worse, than a French heretic, whatever one thought of Henry IV, and was as unacceptable. Even among the people of Paris, the source of some of the most radical of the League supporters, the feeling grew stronger in favor of Henry if he would convert.[250] Religious tradition still remained too strong for them to accept a Protestant king, however.

The League's Estates of 1593 never elected a king. While its delegates fought for their various candidates, Henry IV prepared one of the greatest political moves in history. When factionalism in the Estates was at its height, he announced his intention to reconvert to Catholicism,[251] and on 25 July 1593 he attended Mass and renounced the Huguenot faith. By 27 February 1594 most of France was prepared to accept the coronation of the now Catholic Henry as king of France. The coronation ceremony had to take place at Chartres since the remnants of the League held Reims. A month later Henry IV finally entered his capital city of Paris and on 17 September 1595, after further lengthy negotiations, he gained full absolution from Pope Clement VIII for his previous heretical actions. Support of the Catholic League now clearly carried the stigma of *lèse–majesté*. Since Henry had converted, been absolved by the pope, and crowned King of France, the League's close ties to Spain meant it was supporting a foreign power against a legitimate Catholic French king. That was treason.

---

[249]Isambert, vol. 15, p. 71, no. 51, *Arrêt du parlement séant à Paris qui annulle tous traités faits ou à faire qui appelleraient au trône de France un prince ou une princesse étrangère, comme contraire sà la loi salique et autres lois fondamentales de l'état*, Paris, 28 June 1593. This was the "rump" Parlement of Paris which had become increasingly at odds with the Sixteen. See Shennan, 228–232.
[250]Salmon, "Paris Sixteen," 570.
[251]Jackson, 170–171.

Henry IV further cemented his position as legitimate king by reissuing edicts of his predecessor, such as his 1595 reissuance of Henry III's 1577 Edict of Pacification.[252] His reconversion to Catholicism did not completely end the rebellion, however, as is witnessed by the 1598 *Arrest de la Chambre ordonnee en temps de vacations contre les coulpables de leze Majeste, & perturbateurs de repos public, au pays de Prouence*[253] and the 1599 *Edict dv Roy & Declaration sur les precedents Edicts de Pacification*,[254] but for the majority of Frenchmen, exhausted by years of civil war, the barriers to Henry's legitimacy had now been removed and he was recognized and obeyed as the King of France, even after he issued the Edict of Nantes. France was once again ruled by *un roi* and *une loi*,[255] and even though the Catholic hopes of *une foi* for the French people would not be realized until 1685, it was firmly established that the king of France had to be Catholic. For a Frenchman to fight against Henry IV now was neither defense nor just war, but *lèse-majesté*.

---

[252]*Declaration du Roy sur l'Edict faict par le feu Roy, mil cinq cens soixante dix-sept*, Paris 1595, followed by a reprint of the *Edict de Pacification, faict par le Roy, pour mettre fin aux troubles de son Royaume, & faire desormais viure tous ses subjets en bonne paix & concorde, soubs son obeissance*, published in Parlement 8 October 1577. Both in French Political Pamphlets in the Newberry Library (Lindsay and Neu, no. 1990).

[253]*Arrest de la Chambre ordonnee en temps de vacations contre les coulpables de leze Majeste, & perturbateurs du repos public, au pays de Prouence*, Aix 1598, in French Political Pamphlets in the Newberry Library (Lindsay and Neu, no. 2077).

[254]*Edict dv Roy & Declaration sur les precedents Edicts de Pacification*, published in Parlement 25 February 1599, Paris 1599, in French Political Pamphlets in the Newberry Library (Lindsay and Neu, no. 2112).

[255]At least royal law was united again. The multiplicity of other jurisdictions, especially in local and provincial customary law, remained largely intact until the nineteenth century.

CONCLUSION

Belief in the right to use violence in defense of one's person and property was widespread in sixteenth-century France, but so was the belief in royal authority and the king's obligation to keep order and to protect his people, their property, and their faith. Catholic and Huguenot activists during the Wars of Religion used many biblical and historical sources to support their arguments for resistance, yet they recognized the value of remaining within the prescribed limits of the law when they advocated the use of violence. To achieve this legal justification of what could be viewed as treason, they sought support from the Roman concept of self-defense and the medieval concept of just war. They blended these concepts with French constitutional theories, real or mythic, and created an argument for the right to resist authority when they deemed it to be tyrannical or illegitimate.

Ralph Giesey once wrote, in the context of a discussion of the Huguenot monarchomachs, that "to ignore or dismiss the Huguenot writers' use of Roman Law is to affront their intelligence or their integrity."[256] This statement can be applied equally well to other politico-religious writers in the sixteenth century. The ethical and practical issues which both Huguenot and Catholic resistance writers faced paralleled those which Roman law writers had raised concerning self-defense and sovereignty, and their arguments frequently reflected an understanding of this similarity with the addition of a religio-biblical element. The religious and socioeconomic motivations for their actions have been studied extensively, but until now their use of law in this context has been generally neglected. This study of the legal justification for violence offers valuable insights into the rational side of the political and religious arguments during the Wars of Religion.

---

[256]Giesey, "The Monarchomach Triumvirs," 53.

BIBLIOGRAPHY

I. SOURCE COLLECTIONS

Corpus Juris Canonici Gregorii XIII. Vol. 1, *Decretum Magistri Gratiani*. Graz: Akademische druck-u verlagsanstalt, 1959.

Isambert, F. -A., ed. *Recueil général des anciennes lois françaises. Depuis l'an 420 jusqu'à la révolution de 1789*. 29 vols. Paris 1822–1833.

Laurière, E. -J. et al., eds. *Ordonnances des roys de France de la troisième race: recueillies par ordre chronologique*. 21 vols. Paris: Imprimerie royale, 1723–1849.

Mémoires de Condé, ou Recueil pour servir à l'histoire de France. Contenant ce qui s'est passé de plus memorable dans ce Royaume sous les Regnes de François II et Charles IX. 6 vols. London: Claude du Bosse; J. Nillor et Cies, 1740.

Mémoires de la Ligue, contenant les évenemens les plus remarquables depuis 1576, jusqu'à la paix accordée entre le roi de France & le roi d'Espagne, en 1598. 6 vols. Simon Goulart, ed., new edition edited by Goujet. Amsterdam: Arkstée and Merkus, 1758.

Mémoires de l'Estat de France sous Charles IX. Contenant les choses plus notables, faites & publiées tant par les Catholiques que par ceux de la Religion, depuis de troisiesme Edit de pacification fait au mois d'Aoust 1570, iusques au regne de Henry troisiesme, 3 vols. Simon Goulart, ed. Meidelbourg: Henrich Wolf, 1579.

II. PAMPHLETS AND ROYAL ACTS

Pamphlets and acts which are not cited from published sources are in the Newberry Library collection. Reference numbers are included to the standard listing: Lindsay, Robert O. and John Neu. *French Political Pamphlets 1547–1648: A Catalogue of Major Collections in American Libraries*. Madison: University of Wisconsin Press, 1969.

Advertissement des crimes horribles, commis par les Seditieux Catoliques Romains, Au Pays & Conté du Maine, Depuis le mois de Iuillet 1564, iusques au mois d'Auril 1565. In *Mémoires de Condé*, vol. 6, 367–407.

Advis et Treshvmbles remonstrances à tous Princes, Seigneurs, Cours de Parlemens & suiets de ce Royaume: par vn bon grand nombre de Catholiques, tant de l'Estat Ecclesiastique, la noblesse que tiers Estat, sur la mauuaise & vniuerselle disposition des afaires. 1574. In *Mémoires de l'Estat de France*. Vol. 3, 31–36. Also in French Political Pamphlets in the Newberry Library (Lindsay and Neu, no. 776).

Arrest de la Chambre ordonnee en temps de vacations contre les coulpables de leze Majeste, & perturbateurs de repos public, au pays de Prouence. Aix 1598. In French Political Pamphlets in the Newberry Library (Lindsay and Neu, no. 2077).

Arrest de la Cour de Parlement de Paris contre ceux qui tiennent le party de Henry de Bourbon, declaré heretique par nostre S. Pere le Pape, & qui luy prestent ayde, secours & faueur. Paris 1589. In French Political Pamphlets in the Newberry Library (Lindsay and Neu, no. 1492).

L'Arrest de la court de Parlement publié le dernier iour de Iuin dernier passé, touchant les Rebelles, & perturbateurs du repos & tranquillité des subiects du Roy. Paris 1562. In French Political Pamphlets in the Newberry Library (Lindsay and Neu, no. 277).

Arrest de la covrt des grandz Iours seant en la Ville de Poictiers. Poitiers 1579. In French Political Pamphlets in the Newberry Library (Lindsay and Neu, no. 980).

Arrêt d'une commission présidée par le roi, qui condamne J. Coeur, lui fait grâce de la vie, et confisque ses biens. 19 May 1453. In Isambert, *Recueil général*, vol. 9, no. 214, pp. 254–256.

Arrêt du parlement séant à Paris qui annulle tous traités faits ou à faire qui appelleraient au trône de France un prince ou une princesse étrangère, comme contraire sà la loi salique et autres lois fondamentales de l'état. Paris, 28 June 1593. In Isambert, *Recueil général.* Vol. 15, no. 51, p. 71.

Au Roi, mon souverain seigneur. Sur les miseres du temps present & de la conspiration des Ennemis de sa Majesté. Par un Gentilhomme de l'Eglise. 1586. In *Mémoires de la Ligue*, vol. 2, 100–105.

Bulle de nostre S. Pere le Pape Sixte V, contre Henry de Valois, & ses complices. 1589. In French Political Pamphlets in the Newberry Library (Lindsay and Neu, no. 1421).

Catholique Remonstrance aux Roys et Princes Chrestiens . . . touchant l'abolition des heresies, troubles & scismes qui regnent auiourd'huy en la Chrestienté. 1560. French trans. of Latin text by M. Iean de la Vacquerie. In French Political Pamphlets in the Newberry Library (Lindsay and Neu, no. 212).

Causes qui ont contraint les Catholiques à prendre les armes. 1589. In *Mémoires de la Ligue*, vol. 3, 523–529. Also in French Political Pamphlets in the Newberry Library (Lindsay and Neu, no. 1427).

Declaration. Des causes qui ont mû Monseigneur le Cardinal de Bourbon & les Pairs, Princes, Prelatz, Seigneurs, Villes & Communautez de ce Royaume de veulent subuertir la religion & l'Estat. 1585. In *Mémoires de la Ligue*, vol. 1, 56–63. Also in French Political Pamphlets in the Newberry Library (Lindsay and Neu, no. 1089).

Declaration dv Roy confirmative d'avtre Declaration par luy faicte à son aduenement a la Couronne, de vouloir maintenir & conseruer la Religion Catholique, Apostolique & Romaine. Tours 1591. In French Political Pamphlets in the Newberry Library (Lindsay and Neu, no. 1749).

Declaration du Roy de la cause et occasion de la mort de l'Admiral, & autres ses adherens & complices dernierement advenue en ceste ville de Paris de xxiiii, jour de present mois d'Aoust. Paris 1572. In French Political Pamphlets in the Newberry Library (Lindsay and Neu, no. 729).

Declaration du Roy sur l'Edict faict par le feu Roy, mil cinq cens soixante dix-sept. Paris 1595. Followed by a reprint of the *Edict de Pacification, faict par le Roy, pour mettre fin aux troubles de son Royaume, & faire desormais viure tous ses subjets en bonne paix & concorde, soubs son obeissance,* published in Parlement 8 October 1577. Both in French Political Pamphlets in the Newberry Library (Lindsay and Neu, no. 1990).

Declaration faite par Monseigneur de Duc de Mayenne, Lieutenant-Général de l'Etat & Couronne de France, pour la réunion de tous les Catholiques de ce Roiaume. 1592. In *Mémoires de la Ligue,* vol. 5, 266–277.

Déclaration par laquelle la roi se reconnaît l'auteur du massacre de la Saint-Barthélemy. 28 August 1572. In Isambert, *Recueil général,* vol. 14, part 1, no. 175, pp. 257–259.

Déclaration relative à la confiscation prononcée contre les criminels de lèse majesté. 13 November 1540. In Isambert, *Recueil général,* vol. 12, no. 314, p. 694.

De l'Acord et Remonstrance qve le Roy a faict à tous ses subjectz, qui sont sous son obeissance. Paris, no date, probably 1583. In French Political Pamphlets in the Newberry Library (Lindsay and Neu, no. 1043).

De la Svccession dv droict et prerogative de premier Prince du sang de France, deferée par la loy du Royaume, à Monseigneur Charles Cardinal de Bourbon, par le mort de Monseigneur François de Valois Duc d'Anjou. In French from the Latin treatise of Matthew Zampini, *Pro svccessione praerogativae primi principis, per legem Regni, Cardinali Borbonio delatae.* Paris 1589. Both in French Political Pamphlets in the Newberry Library (Lindsay and Neu, nos. 1668 and 1669).

Discovrs d'vn vertvevx Catholiqve qvi est vne iuste & vraye deffense de la Maiesté tres-Chrestienne & ample response contre ses capitaux ennemis; des heretiques du iourd'huy, leurs grandes & atroces iniures, calomnies, maldisances, trahisons, machinations, & coniurations tresiniques & desseins fort à craindre & à redouter. 1587. In French Political Pamphlets in the Newberry Library (Lindsay and Neu, no. 1165).

Discovrs svr le Droit Pretendu par ceux de Guise sur la Couronne de France. 1583. In French Political Pamphlets in the Newberry Library (Lindsay and Neu, no. 1054).

Discovrs Sur les causes de l'execution faite és personnes de ceux qui auoient coniure contre le Roy & son Estat. Paris 1572. In French Political Pamphlets in the Newberry Library (Lindsay and Neu, no. 723).

Discovrs svr les occvrrences des gverres intestines de ce Royavme, et de la ivstice de Dieu contre le rebelles au Roy, & comme de droict divin, est licite à sa maiesté punir ses subiets, pour la Religion violée. Paris 1572. In French Political Pamphlets in the Newberry Library (Lindsay and Neu, no. 724).

Edit de Janvier de 1562. In *Mémoires de Condé,* vol. 3, 1–11. Also in French Political Pamphlets in the Newberry Library (Lindsay and Neu, no. 284).

Edict de Pacification faict par le Roy pour mettre fin aux Troubles de son Royaume, & faire desormais viure tous ses subiects en bonne paix, vnion & concorde, soubs son obeissance. Published in Parlement 8 October 1577. Paris 1578. Reissued 1595. In the French Political Pamphlets in the Newberry Library (Lindsay and Neu, no. 939 and the reissue, no. 1990).

Edict dv Roy & Declaration sur les precedents Edicts de Pacification. Published in Parlement 25 February 1599. Paris 1599. In French Political Pamphlets in the Newberry Library (Lindsay and Neu, no. 2112).

Edict dv Roy, Contenant restablissement des Edicts de Pacification faicts par le deffunct Roy Henry, troisiesme sur les troubles de ce Royaume. Published by the Cour de Parlement sitting at Challons, 24 July 1591. In French Political Pamphlets in the Newberry Library (Lindsay and Neu, no. 1750).

Edit du roi, sur la Defense des armes, qu'il fait contre se sont ligués en son Royaume. 28 March 1585. In *Mémoires de la Ligue,* vol. 1, 54–56.

Edict du Roy sur la Pacification des troubles, contenant confirmation, ampliation, & declaration, tant des precedents Edicts sur ledit faict, mesmes en l'an 1577, que des Articles arrestez en la Conference de Nerac. 26 January 1581, Paris. In French Political Pamphlets in the Newberry Library (Lindsay and Neu, no. 1011).

Edict dv Roy svr la Pacification des troubles de ce Royaume. 11 August 1573. Paris 1573. In French Political Pamphlets in the Newberry Library (Lindsay and Neu, no. 755).

Edict dv Roy svr la revocation des edicts de la Ligue, faits és années mil cinq cens quatre vingts cinq, & quatre vingts huict. Tours 1591. In French Political Pamphlets in the Newberry Library (Lindsay and Neu, no. 1751).

Edit portant confiscation au profit du roi des biens de ceux qui seront condamnés comme criminels de lèse-majesté, et portant que la confiscation s'étendra tant sur les biens personnels du condamné que sur les fiefs inférieurs et sur les meubles, nonobstant toutes substitutions. 10 August 1539. In Isambert, *Recueil général,* vol. 12, no. 285, pp. 590–591.

Edit portant que les receleurs de luthériens seront punis des mêmes peines qu'eux s'ils ne les livrent à la justice; et que les dénonciateurs auront le quart des confiscations. Paris, 29 January 1534; registered by the Parlement of Paris on February 1. In Isambert, *Recueil général,* vol. 12, no. 211, pp. 402–403.

Edit qui révoque ceux de pacification, et qui enjoint à tous les sujets du roi de professer la religion catholique. July 1585. In Isambert, *Recueil général,* vol. 14, part II, no. 290, p. 595. Also in *Mémoires de la Ligue,* vol. 1, 178–182.

Edict sur la pacification des troubles du royaume, les protestants, les religionnaires fugitifs, la convocation des Estates-Généraux . . . May 1576. Isambert, *Recueil général*, vol. 14, part II, no. 46, pp. 280–302. Also appears as *Edict dv Roy svr la Pacification des trovbles de ce Royaume*. May 1576. In French Political Pamphlets in the Newberry Library (Lindsay and Neu, no. 881).

Exhortation et Remonstrance, faite d'vn commvn accord par les françois Catholiques & Pacifiques, pour la paix. 1586. In French Political Pamphlets in the Newberry Library (Lindsay and Neu, no. 1150).

Ivstification de la gverre entreprise, commencee et povrsvivie sovz la conducte de tres-valeureux & debonnaire Prince Monseigneur le Duc de Mayenne. Paris 1589. In French Political Pamphlets in the Newberry Library (Lindsay and Neu, no. 1546).

Legitime conseil des Roys de France pendant leur iuvne aage, Contre ceux qui veulent maintenir l'illegitime gouuernement de ceux de Guise, soubz le tiltre de la Maiorité du Roy. . . . 1560? In *Mémoires de Condé*, vol. 1, 225–256.

Lettre de Monsieur le Prince de Condé, avx églises reformees de France. 7 April 1562. In *Mémoires de Condé*, vol. 3, 172–173.

Lettres d'abolition en faveur de ceux qui n'ont pas révélé à la justice les biens de Jacques Coeur. 11 May 1459. In Isambert, *Recueil général*, vol. 9, no. 248, pp. 361–363.

Lettres qui mettent Geoffroi Coeur en possession des terres et domaines confisqués sur Jacques Coeur son père. August 1463. In Isambert, *Recueil général*, vol. 9, no. 55, pp. 469–472.

Lettres pour comprendre au a) Traité d'Arras b) Jacques de Savoie c) Marie de Luxembourg sa femme d) et Françoise soeur de Marie; Restitution ordonnée des Biens confisqués sur leur aïeul. 28 January 1484. In Laurière, *Ordonnances des roys de France*, vol. 19, pp. 458–461.

Protestation et Declaration dv Roy de Nauarre, sur la venue de son armee en France. 1587. In French Political Pamphlets in the Newberry Library (Lindsay and Neu, no. 1185).

Remonstrance a tovs estats. Par laquelle est en brief demonstré la foy & innocence des vrays Chrestiens. 1561? In *Mémoires de Condé*, vol. 2, 834–863.

Remonstrance av Roy Henry III, du nom, Roy de France & de Pologne, & aux Estats generaux de France à Bloys. Faict par le sieur de Sindré, l'vn des deputez de la Noblesse de Bourbonnois. Lyon 1589. In French Political Pamphlets in the Newberry Library (Lindsay and Neu, no. 1649).

Remonstrance avx François svr levr sedition, rebellion et felonnie, contre la Majesté du Roy. 1589. In French Political Pamphlets in the Newberry Library (not listed in Lindsay and Neu).

Remonstrance de Monseignevr le Prince de Condé et ses associez à la Royne, Sur le iugement de rebellion donné contre eux par leurs ennemis, se disans estre la Cour de Parlement de Paris. . . . In *Mémoires de Condé*, vol. 3, 404–427.

Remontrance envoyee au Roy, par la noblesse de la Religion reformee du Païs et Conté du Maine. Presented to the king at Roussillon 10 August 1564. In *Mémoires de Cónde*, vol. 6, 327–366.

Responce avx Declarations & protestations de Messieurs de Guise, faictes sous le nom de Monseigneur le Cardinal de Bourbon, pour justifier leur iniuste prise des armes. 1585. In French Political Pamphlets in the Newberry Library (Lindsay and Neu, no. 1116).

Response av livre inscrit povr la maiorité dv Roy Francois II. 1560. In *Mémoires de Condé*, vol. 1, 169–205.

Responce à la svpplication, contre celvy lequel faisant semblant de donner aduis au Roy de se faire Catholic veult exciter ses bons subiects à rebellion. 1591. In French Political Pamphlets in the Newberry Library (Lindsay and Neu, no. 1762).

Svpplication et Remonstrance addressee av Roy de Navarre & autres Princes du Sang de France, pour la deliurance du Roy & du Royaume. 1560? In *Mémoires de Condé*, vol. 1, 257–318.

Traicte D'Association faicte par Mon-Seignevr le Prince de Condé auec les Princes, Cheualiers de l'ordre, Seigneurs, Capitaines, Gentils-hommes, & autres . . . pour maintenir l'honneur de Dieu, le repos de ce Royaume, & l'estat & liberté du Roy, sous le gouuernement de la Royne sa mere. 1562. In French Political Pamphlets in the Newberry Library (Lindsay and Neu, no. 271).

Traitte Dv Qvel on pevt apprendre en quel cas il est permis à l'homme Chrestien de porter les armes et par leqvel est respondu à Pierre Charpentier, tendant à fin d'empescher la paix, & nous laisser la guerre. Par Pierre Fabre à Monsieur de Lomainie, Baron de Terride, & de Seriniac, translated from Latin. 1576. In French Political Pamphlets in the Newberry Library (Lindsay and Neu, no. 877).

III. OTHER PRIMARY SOURCES

Beaumanoir, Philippe de Remi, sire de. *Coutumes de Beauvaisis*. Salmon, A., editor. 2 vols. Paris: A. Picard et fils, 1899–1900.

Belloy, Pierre de. (Also attributed to Edmond de Lalouette). *Apologie Catholiqve contre les libelles declarations, advis, et consvltations faictes, escrites, & publiees par les Liguez Perturbateurs du repos du Royaume de France: qui se sont esleuez depuis le deces de feu Monseigneur frere vnique du Roy*. N.p. 1585.

Bèze, Théodore de. *Du droit des magistrats*. Edited by Robert M. Kingdon. Geneva: Librairie Droz, 1970.

Bodin, Jean. *Six Books of a Commonweale*. Richard Knolles, translator, 1606. Rp. Cambridge: Harvard University Press, 1962.

Boucher, Jean. *De iusta Henri Tertii: Abdicatione e francorum regno*. 2nd ed. Paris: N. Niuellium, 1589.

Bracton, Henry de. *De Legibus et Consuetudinibus Angliae*. 4 vols. G. E. Woodbine, ed. New Haven: Yale University Press, 1915–1942.

Hotman, François. *Francogallia*. Variorum edition. Latin text by Ralph E. Giesey, translated by J. H. M. Salmon. Cambridge: Cambridge University Press, 1972.

———. *P. Sixti V. Fvlmen Brvtum. In Henricvm sereniss, Regem Nauarrae, & illustriss Henricvm Borbonium, Principem olim Conaeum, euibratum*. N.p. 1586.

Pasquier, Etienne. *L'interprétation des Institutes de Justinian*. Paris, 1847; Rp. Geneva: Slatkine Reprints, 1970.

Vindiciae contra tyrannos. French translation of 1581. Edited by A. Jouanna *et al*. Geneva: Librairie Droz, 1979.

IV. SECONDARY SOURCES

Allen, John William. *A History of Political Thought in the Sixteenth Century*. New York: Dial Press, Inc., 1928.

Armstrong, E. *The French Wars of Religion: Their Political Aspect*. London: Percival and Co., 1904.

Aubépin, M. H. *De l'influence de Dumoulin sur la législation française*. Vol. 1. Paris: Libraire du conseil d'Etat, 1855.

Barnavi, Eli. *Le Parti de Dieu: Etude sociale et politique des chefs de la Ligue parisienne, 1585–1594*. Brussels: Editions Nauwelaerts, 1980.

Baumgartner, Fréderic. *Radical Reactionaries: the Political Thought of the French Catholic League*. Geneva: Droz, 1975.

Beame, E. M. "The Limits of Toleration in Sixteenth-Century France." *Studies in the Renaissance* 13 (1966): 250–265.

Benedict, Philip. "The Saint Bartholomew's Massacres in the Provinces." *Historical Journal* 21 (June 1978): 205–225.

Billacois, François. *Duel dans la société française des XVIe–XVIIe siècles: Essai de psychosociologie historique*. Paris: Editions de l'Ecole des haute études en sciences sociales, 1986.

Bourgeon, Jean-Louis. "Pour une histoire, enfin, de la Saint-Barthélemy." *Revue historique* 171 (July–September, 1989): 83–142.

Brissaud, Jean B. *A History of French Public Law*. South Hackensack, New Jersey: Rothman Reprints, 1969.

Brundage, James A. "The Holy War and Medieval Lawyers." In *The Holy War*, ed. Thomas Patrick Murphy, 99–140. Columbus: Ohio State University Press, 1976.

Caprariis, Vittorio de. *Propaganda e pensiero politico in Francia durante le guerre di religione*. Vol. 1, *1559–1572*. Naples: Edizioni scientifiche italiane, 1959.

Chalambert, Victor de. *Histoire de la Ligue sous les règnes de Henri III et Henri IV, ou quinze années de l'histoire de France*. Paris 1898; Rp. Geneva: Slatkine-Megariotis, 1974.

Chartier, Roger. *The Cultural Uses of Print in Early Modern France*. Princeton: Princeton University Press, 1987.

Church, William Farr. *Constitutional Thought in Sixteenth-Century France: A Study in the Evolution of Ideas*. Cambridge: Harvard University Press, 1941.

Coville, Alfred. *Jean Petit: La question du tyrannicide au commencement du XVe siècle*. Paris, 1932; Rp. Geneva: Slatkine Reprints, 1974.

Crouzet, Denis. *Les guerriers de Dieu. La violence au temps des troubles de religion (vers 1525–vers 1610)*, 2 vols. Seyssel: Champ Vallon, 1990.

Cuénin, Micheline. *Le duel sous l'Ancien Régime*. Paris: Presses de la Renaissance, 1982.

Cuttler, S. H. *Law of Treason and Treason Trials in Later Medieval France*. Cambridge: Cambridge University Press, 1981.

Davis, Natalie Zemon. *Fiction in the Archives: Pardon Tales and Their Tellers in Sixteenth-Century France*. Stanford: Stanford University Press, 1987.

———. "The Rites of Violence: Religious Riot in Sixteenth-Century France." *Past and Present* 59 (1973): 51–91.

Descimon, Robert. *Qui étaient les sieze? Mythes et réalités de la Ligue parisienne*. Paris: Fédération Paris et Ile de France, 1983.

Diefendorf, Barbara. *Beneath the Cross: Catholics and Huguenots in Sixteenth-Century Paris*. New York: Oxford University Press, 1991.

Eire, Carlos M. N. *War against the Idols: The Reformation of Worship from Erasmus to Calvin*. New York: Cambridge University Press, 1986.

Giesey, Ralph E. "The Juristic Basis of the Dynastic Right to the French Throne." *Transactions of the American Philosophical Society* 51, pt. 5 (1961): 1–47.

———. "The Monarchomach Triumvirs: Hotman, Beza, and Mornay." *Bibliothèque d'humanisme et renaissance* 32 (January 1970): 41–56.

———. "When and Why Hotman Wrote the *Francogallia*." *Bibliothèque d'Humanisme et Renaissance* 29 (1967): 581–611.

Hale, J. R. *War and Society in Renaissance Europe, 1450–1620*. Baltimore: Johns Hopkins University Press, 1985.

Hanley Sarah. "The *Discours Politiques* in Monarchomach Ideology: Resistance Right in Sixteenth-Century France." In *Assemblee di Stati e Istituzioni Rappresentative nella Storia del Pensiero Politico Moderno*, 121–134. Perugia: Annali della Facoltà di Scienze Politiche, 1982.

———. "Engendering the State: Family Formation and State Building in Early Modern France." *French Historical Studies* 16 (Spring 1989): 4–27.

———. "The French Constitution Revised: Representative Assemblies and Resistance Right in the Sixteenth Century." In *Society and Institutions in Early Modern France*, ed. Mack P. Holt, 36–50. Athens: University of Georgia Press, 1991.

———. *The 'Lit de Justice' of the Kings of France: Constitutional Ideology in Legend, Ritual, and Discourse*. Princeton: Princeton University Press, 1983.

Heller, Henry. *Iron and Blood: Civil Wars in Sixteenth-Century France*. Montreal: McGill-Queen's University Press, 1991.

Holt, Mack P. *The Duke of Anjou and the Politique Struggle during the Wars of Religion*. Cambridge: Cambridge University Press, 1986.

Jackson, Richard A. "Elective Kingship and *Consensus Populi* in Sixteenth-Century France." *Journal of Modern History* 44 (June 1972): 155–171.

Johnson, James Turner. *Ideology, Reason, and the Limitation of War: Religious and Secular Concepts 1200–1740*. Princeton: Princeton University Press, 1975.

———. *Just War Tradition and the Restraint of War—A Moral and Historical Inquiry.* Princeton: Princeton University Press, 1981.

Jouanna, Arlette. *Le Devoir de révolte: La Noblesse française et la question de l'état moderne, 1559–1661.* Paris: Fayard, 1989.

Kaeuper, Richard W. *War, Justice, and Public Order: England and France in the Later Middle Ages.* New York: Oxford University Press, 1988.

Keen, Maurice. *The Laws of War in the Late Middle Ages.* London: Routledge and K. Paul, 1965.

Kelley, Donald R. *The Beginning of Ideology: Consciousness and Society in the French Reformation.* Cambridge: Cambridge University Press, 1981.

———. *François Hotman: A Revolutionary's Ordeal.* Princeton: Princeton University Press, 1973.

———. "Martyrs, Myths, and the Massacre: the Background of St. Bartholomew." *American Historical Review* 77 (December 1972): 1323–1342.

Kingdon, Robert M. *Myths about the St. Bartholomew's Day Massacres, 1572–1576.* Cambridge: Harvard University Press, 1988.

Lander, J. R. "Attainder and Forfeiture 1453–1509." *Historical Journal* 4 (1961): 119–151.

Lemaire, André. *Les Lois Fondamentales de la monarchie française d'après les théoreciens de l'ancien régime.* Paris: E. Thorn et fils, 1907; Rp. Geneva: Slatkine–Megariotis Reprints, 1975.

Major, J. Russell. *Representative Government in Early Modern France.* New Haven: Yale University Press, 1980.

———. *Representative Institutions in Renaissance France, 1421–1559.* Madison, Wisconsin: University of Wisconsin Press, 1960.

Meaux, Marie Camille Alfred, Vicomte de. *Les luttes religieuses en France au seizième siècle.* Paris: E. Plon et Cie, 1879.

Mesnard, Pierre. *L'essor de la philosophie politique au XVIe siècle.* 3rd ed. Paris: J. Vrin, 1969.

Meyer, Gert. "Charles Dumoulin. Ein führender französischer Rechts Gelehrter." *Rechts-und sozial wissenschaftliche Vorträge und Schriften* 4 (Nuremburg, 1956): 11–74.

Mousset, Albert. "Les droits de l'infante Isabelle-Claire-Eugénie à la couronne de France." *Bulletin hispanique* 16 (1914): 46–79.

Muchembled, Robert. *La Violence au village: Sociabilité et comportements populaires en Artois du XVe au XVIIe siècle.* Paris: Hachette, 1977.

Musto, Ronald G. *The Catholic Peace Tradition.* Maryknoll, NY: Orbis, 1986.

Neuschel, Kristen B. *Word of Honor: Interpreting Noble Culture in Sixteenth-Century France.* Ithaca, New York: Cornell University Press, 1989.

Perrot, Ernest. *Arresta communia Scacarii, deux collections d'arrêts notables de l'Echiquier de Normandie.* Caen: L. Jouan, 1910.

———. *Les cas royaux: origine et développement de la théorie aux XIIIe et XIVe siècles.* 1910; Rp., Geneva: Slatkine-Megariotis, 1975.

Pissard, Hippolyte. *La clameur de haro dans le droit normand.* Caen: L. Jouan, 1911.

——. *La Guerre Sainte en pays chrétien; essai sur l'origine et le développement des théories canoniques*. Paris: A. Picard et fils, 1912.

Regout, Robert. *La doctrine de la guerre juste de Saint Augustin à nos jours*. Paris: A. Pedone, 1935.

Repgen, Konrad. "What is 'Religious War'?" In *Politics and Society in Reformation Europe: Essays for Sir Geoffrey Elton on His Sixty-fifth Birthday*, eds., E. I. Kouri and Tom Scott, 311–328. New York: Macmillan, 1987.

Rowan, Steven. "Ulrich Zasius and John Eck: 'Faith need not be kept with an enemy'." *Sixteenth Century Journal* 8 (Summer 1977): 79–95.

——. "Ulrich Zasius and the Baptism of Jewish Children." *Sixteenth Century Journal* 6 (October 1973): 3–25.

Russell, Frederick H. *The Just War in the Middle Ages*. Cambridge: Cambridge University Press, 1975.

Salmon, J. H. M. *The French Religious Wars in English Political Thought*. Oxford: Clarendon Press, 1959.

——. "The Paris Sixteen, 1584–94: The Social Analysis of a Revolutionary Movement." *Journal of Modern History* 44 (December 1972): 540–576.

Sambuc, Jean. "Documents sur la réforme dans le Comtat et en Provence." *Bulletin de la Société de l'histoire du protestantisme française*. 117 (1971): 629–636.

Shennan, J. H. *The Parlement of Paris*. Ithaca: Cornell University Press, 1968.

Skinner, Quentin. *The Foundations of Modern Political Thought*. Vol. 2, *The Age of Reformation*. New York: Cambridge University Press, 1978.

——. "The Origins of the Calvinist Theory of Revolution." In *After the Reformation: Essays in Honor of J. H. Hexter*, ed. Barbara C. Malament, 309–330. Philadelphia: University of Pennsylvania Press, 1980.

Smither, James R. "The St. Bartholomew's Day Massacre and Images of Kingship in France, 1572–1574." *The Sixteenth Century Journal* 22 (Spring 1991): 27–46.

Strayer, Joseph R. "The Writ of Novel Disseisin in Normandy at the end of the Thirteenth Century." In *Medieval Statecraft and the Perspectives of History*, 3–12. Princeton: Princeton University Press, 1971.

Struckmeyer, Frederick. "The 'Just War' and the Right of Self-Defense." *Ethics* 82 (October 1971): 48–55.

Sullivan, Shaun J., O.F.M. *Killing in Defense of Private Property: The Development of a Roman Catholic Moral Teaching, Thirteenth to Eighteenth Centuries*. Missoula, Montana: Scholars Press, 1976.

Sutherland, Donald W. *The Assize of Novel Disseisin*. Oxford: Clarendon Press, 1973.

Sutherland, Nicola M. *The Huguenot Struggle for Recognition*. New Haven: Yale University Press, 1980.

——. *Massacre of St. Bartholomew and the European Conflict 1559–1572*. New York: Barnes and Noble, 1973.

Teichman, Jenny. *Pacifism and the Just War*. Oxford: Basil Blackwell, 1986.

Timbal, P. -C. "La confiscation dans le droit français des XIIIe et XIVe siècles." *Revue historique de droit français et étranger* 4th ser. 22 (1943): 44–79 and 4th ser. 22 (1944): 35–60.

Turchetti, Mario. "Religious Concord and Political Tolerance in Sixteenth- and Seventeenth-Century France." *Sixteenth Century Journal* 22 (Spring 1991): 15–25.

Vanderpol, Alfred. *La doctrine scolastique du droit de guerre.* Paris: A. Pedone, 1925.

Villey, Michel. *La croisade: Essai sur la formation d'une théorie juridique.* Paris: Vrin, 1942.

Walzer, Michael. *Just and Unjust Wars: A Moral Argument with Historical Illustrations.* New York: Basic Books, 1977.

Weill, Georges. *Les théories sur le pouvoir royal en France pendant les guerres de religion.* Paris 1891; Rp. Geneva: Slatkine Reprints, 1971.

Wells, Donald A. "How Much Can the 'Just War' Justify?" *Journal of Philosophy* 66 (December 1969): 819–829.

Yardeni, Myriam. *La conscience nationale en France pendant les guerres de religion (1559–1598).* Louvain: Editions Nauwelaerts, 1971.

INDEX

76

www.ingramcontent.com/pod-product-compliance
Lightning Source LLC
Chambersburg PA
CBHW050349110426
42812CB00008B/2419